SCIENCE WORKSHOP SERIES

EARTH SCIENCE

Geology

with an Introduction to Scientific Method

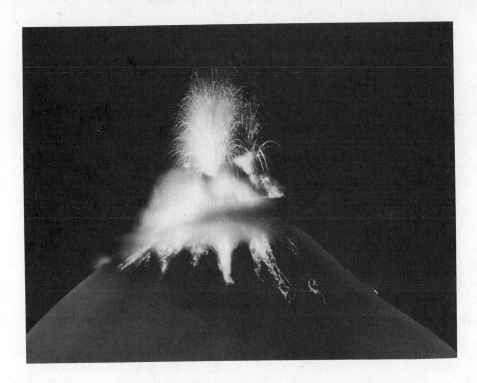

Seymour Rosen

GLOBE BOOK COMPANY
A Division of Simon & Schuster
Englewood Cliffs, New Jersey

THE AUTHOR

Seymour Rosen received his B.A. and M.S. degrees from Brooklyn College. He taught science in the New York City School System for twenty-seven years. Mr. Rosen was also a contributing participant in a teacher-training program for the development of science curriculum for the New York City Board of Education.

Cover Photograph: UPI/Bettman Newsphotos
Photo Researcher: Rhoda Sidney

Photo Credits:

p. 53, Fig. A: Arthur Mina
p. 53, Fig. B: Arthur Mina
p. 53, Fig. C: Arthur Mina
p. 53, Fig. D: Arthur Mina
p. 74: Marshall Space Flight Center/NASA
p. 80, Fig. E: Alvin E. Staffan/Photo Researchers
p. 89, Fig. A: American Airlines
p. 104, Fig. D: Swiss National Tourist Office
p. 116, Fig. D: Gale Zucker/Stock, Boston
p. 139, Fig. B: Alan Pitcairn/Grant Heilman
p. 145, Fig. A: Rob Crandall/Stock, Boston
p. 181, Fig. A: Topham/The Image Works
p. 181, Fig. B: UPI/Bettmann Newsphotos
p. 183, Fig. E: Beaver Valley Nuclear Complex
p. 192: Paul Conklin/Monkmeyer Press

ISBN: 0-8359-0377-0

Printed in the United States of America
7 8 9 10 00 99

Globe Book Company
A Division of Simon & Schuster
Englewood Cliffs, New Jersey

CONTENTS

Introduction to Earth Science

Have you ever wondered what the inside of the earth is really like? Or what causes an earthquake, or a volcanic eruption? Have you ever wondered how mountains form, or why scientists study dinosaur remains? In this book, you will learn answers to these questions. You will learn important facts about the earth and how it changes — changes that affect the world we live in.

In this book, you will study the parts of the earth's surface. The rocks and minerals that make up the earth's surface are covered. You may already know that each day people dig and drill to take some valuable minerals such as gold from the earth's surface. Ways that the earth's surface is constantly being changed also are explained. Rivers, waves, wind — what do they all have in common? They all wear away some parts of the earth and build up others. And you will learn how pollution is changing the earth. Perhaps, you will think of ways to help stop pollution.

Remember, the earth is slowly changing even as you read this page. Now you can begin to find out how.

How do scientists measure things?

1

area: measure of the size of a surface
length: distance between two points
mass: amount of matter in an object
temperature: measure of how hot or cold something is
volume: measure of the amount of space an object takes up
weight: measure of the pull of gravity on an object

LESSON 1 | How do scientists measure things?

How much do you weigh? What is your height? How many tiles will cover your kitchen floor? How much milk should be added to a cake mix? What is the temperature outside? All of these questions are answered by measurements.

Measuring is an important part of daily life. People use measurements all the time—for shopping, cooking, construction, and deciding how warm to dress. Measuring also is an important part of science.

A measurement has two parts: a <u>number</u> and a <u>unit</u>. A unit is a standard amount used to measure something.

EXAMPLES
        100 grams   25 liters

        number standard   number standard
               unit   unit

There are many kinds of measurements. The most common are:

MASS and weight are related, but they are not the same. **Mass** is a measure of the amount of matter in an object. **Weight** is a measure of the pull of gravity on an object. The basic unit of mass in the metric system is the kilogram (kg). Mass is measured with a balance.

LENGTH is the distance from one point to another as measured by a ruler. The basic metric unit of length is the <u>meter</u> (m). You can use a meter stick or metric ruler to measure length.

AREA is a measure of <u>surface</u> room—how big something is in two directions. You can find the area of a rectangle by multiplying its length by its width. Area is measured in square units, such as square meters (m^2).

VOLUME is the measure of the amount of <u>space</u> an object takes up—how big an object is in all three directions. The <u>liter</u> (L) is the basic unit of volume in the metric system. A <u>measuring cup</u> or a <u>graduated cylinder</u> is used to measure the volume of liquids.

The volume of a solid can be measured in cubic centimeters (cm^3). You can find the volume of a cube or rectangle by multiplying its length by its width by its height. 1000 cubic centimeters equals 1 liter.

TEMPERATURE is the measure of how hot or cold an object is. Temperature is measured with a thermometer in <u>degrees</u> <u>Celsius</u> ºC, or <u>degrees</u> <u>Fahrenheit</u> ºF. The Celsius scale usually is used in science.

UNDERSTANDING METRICS

In the United States, people usually use <u>English</u> units of measurement such as, <u>ounces</u>, <u>pounds</u>, <u>inches</u> and <u>feet</u>. Most other countries use <u>metric</u> units. Metric units include the <u>gram</u>, <u>kilogram</u>, <u>meter</u>, and <u>centimeter</u>. Scientists also use the metric system. In science, you will use mostly metric units.

The metric system is based upon units of <u>ten</u>. Each unit is ten times smaller or larger than the next unit. This means that a unit is made <u>larger</u> by <u>multiplying</u> it by <u>10</u> and made <u>smaller</u> by <u>dividing</u> by <u>10</u>. Prefixes describe a unit's value. The prefixes and their meanings are listed below.

PREFIX	MEANING	
kilo- [KILL-uh] ———— one thousand (1,000)		each, larger
hecto- [HEC-tuh]———— one hundred (100)		by a multiple
deca- [DEC-uh] ———— ten (10)		of <u>ten</u>
deci- [DESS-ih] ———— one tenth (1/10)		each, smaller
centi- [SEN-tih] ———— one hundredth (1/100)		by a multiple
milli- [MILL-ih] ———— one thousandth (1/1,000)		of 1/10

Use the chart above to answer the following questions.

1. To change from tens to hundreds, you multiply by ——————— .

1, 10, 100

2. To change from hundreds to thousands, you multiply by ——————— .

1, 10, 100

3. In the metric system, to change from one unit to the next higher unit, what must you do? ———————

4. To change from one unit to the next <u>lower</u> unit, you must divide by ——————— .

1, 10, 100

5. Which prefix stands for a <u>greater</u> value?

   a) deca- or kilo-? ———————   **d)** hecto- or kilo-? ———————

   b) kilo- or milli-? ———————   **e)** centi- or deci-? ———————

   c) centi- or milli-? ———————   **f)** deca- or deci-? ———————

MEASURING MASS

1. In the metric system, the unit of <u>mass</u> is the _____ .
   meter, kilogram, pound

2. Mass and weight _____ the same.
   are, are not

3. _____ is a measure of the amount of matter in an object.
   mass, weight

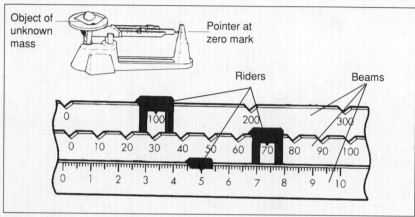

Figure A

4. What instrument is used to measure mass?_____

5. What is the mass of the object shown?_____

TRUE OR FALSE

In the space provided, write "true" if the sentence is true. Write "false" if the sentence is false.

_____ 1. Weight is a measure of the pull of gravity on an object.

_____ 2. Scientists use English units of measurement.

_____ 3. The prefix centi- stands for one hundredth (1/100).

_____ 4. A graduate is used to measure mass.

_____ 5. The basic unit of length in the metric system is the meter.

_____ 6. Volume is a measure of the amount of matter in an object.

_____ 7. One kilogram is less than one gram.

_____ 8. A measurement has two parts.

_____ 9. A unit is an amount used to measure something.

_____ 10. Most countries use the metric system.

4

MEASURING LENGTH

Length is measured with a metric ruler. Part of a combined metric and inch ruler is shown in Figure B. On the metric side of the ruler the distance between numbered lines is equal to one centimeter. Each centimeter is divided into 10 equal parts. Each one of these parts is equal to one millimeter.

The figure below shows a combined metric and inch ruler.

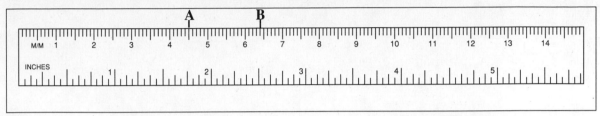

Figure B

1. What value does the prefix <u>milli-</u> stand for? _____

2. What value does the prefix <u>centi-</u> stand for? _____

3. Which is <u>larger</u>, a meter or a millimeter? _____

4. How many millimeters make 1 centimeter? _____

5. The length at A may be written as 45 mm. It may also be written as _____ .
   45 cm, 4.5 cm, 4.5 mm

6. The length at B may be written as _____ mm or _____ cm.

Measure each of the following lengths. Write the lengths on the right in centimeters and millimeters.

7. —————————————————————   7. _____ cm _____ mm

8. ————————————————   8. _____ cm _____ mm

9. —————   9. _____ cm _____ mm

10. ———————————————————————   10. _____ cm _____ mm

To the right of each length listed, <u>draw</u> a line of that length.

a) 92 mm

b) 9.2 cm

c) 43 mm

d) 3.5 cm

MEASURING AREA

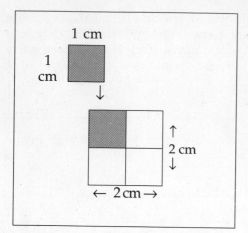

Figure C

The square in Figure C has an area of 2 square centimeters (2 cm²).

Area= 1 × l₂

    = 2 cm × 2 cm

Area= 4 square centimeters (4cm²).

Figure the area of each of the following rectangles: (Measure Figures G and H yourself.)

4 cm

2cm

Figure D

_____

3 cm

1cm

Figure E

_____

4 cm

3cm

Figure F

_____

Figure G

_____

Figure H

_____

CALCULATING AREA

Find the areas of the following rectangles:

1. 5 meters × 5 meters_____

2. 2.5 cm × 5 cm _____

3. 10 millimeters × 10 millimeters_____

MEASURING VOLUME

The volume of liquids is measured in a <u>graduated cylinder</u>. A graduated cylinder is a glass tube that is marked with divisions to show the amount of liquid in it. To measure liquid volume, you hold the graduated cylinder at your <u>eye level</u>. The surface of the liquid will have a "belly-down" curve. You should read the mark that lines up with the <u>bottom</u> of the curve.

What is the liquid volume in this graduated cylinder?

_____

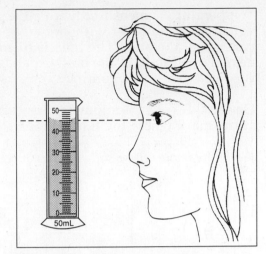

Figure I

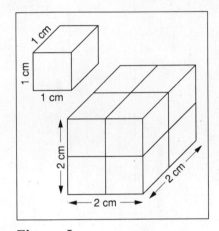

Figure J

What is the volume of a cube that is 2 cm × 2 cm × 2 cm?

$$\text{Volume} = l_1 \times l_2 \times l_3$$

$$= 2 \text{ cm} \times 2 \text{ cm} \times 2 \text{ cm}$$

$$\text{Volume} = 8 \text{ cubic centimeters } (8\text{cm}^3).$$

Find the volume of each of the following rectangles:

<u>Volume</u>

1. 2 cm × 5 cm × 1 cm   _____

2. 8 m × 2 m × 2 m   _____

3. 1 mm × 1 mm × 10 mm _____

4. 4 cm × 2 cm × 3 cm   _____

5. 5 m × 3 m × 6 m   _____

READING A CELSIUS THERMOMETER

Temperature is measured with a thermometer. Many thermometers, including the ones you are most familiar with, are made of glass tubes. At the bottom of the tube is a wider part called the bulb. The bulb is filled with a liquid, such as mercury. When the bulb is heated, the liquid in the bulb expands, or gets larger. It rises in the tube. When the bulb is cooled, the liquid contracts, or gets smaller. It falls in the tube.

On the sides of a thermometer are a series of marks. You read the temperature by looking at the mark where the liquid stops.

Write the temperature shown on each celsius thermometer in the space provided.

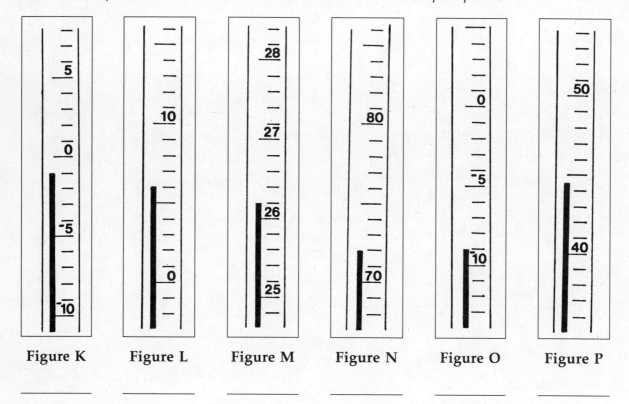

Figure K	Figure L	Figure M	Figure N	Figure O	Figure P
_____	_____	_____	_____	_____	_____

REACHING OUT

One cubic centimeter is equal to one millimeter (mL). How many <u>liters</u> of water can a 1800 cm³ pan hold? _____

8

What is scientific method?

2

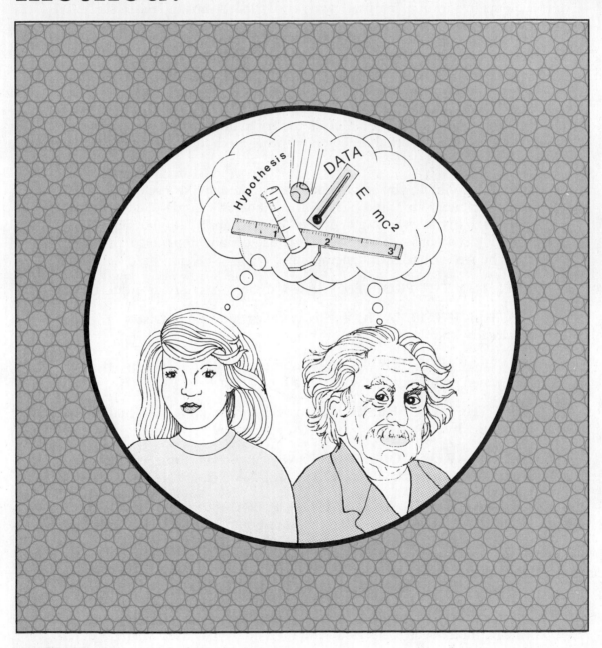

data [DAYT-uh]:   record of observations
hypothesis [hy-PAHTH-uh-sis]:   suggested solution to a problem based upon known
   information
scientific method: problem solving guide

LESSON 2 | What is scientific method?

You may not realize it, but you do problem-solving every day. You do not always think about how to solve a particular problem. You solve problems in sort of a "natural" way, a way that seems to "make sense." And it usually does.

For example, suppose you put your key into your house door and try to turn it, but it does not budge. You wonder what's wrong. You examine the key to make certain that it is the correct one. Then you try again. The key still does not turn. What next? You might "jiggle" the key. Or, you might pull back on the door knob as you try to turn the key. One of these approaches <u>might</u> work. If not, you try other methods until the problem is solved.

Without knowing it, you solve problems very much like a scientist does. You use **scientific method**. Scientific method is a guide used to solve problems. It involves asking questions, making observations, and trying things out in an orderly way. Scientists use certain steps to solve problems. The steps of scientific method are:

- **IDENTIFY THE PROBLEM**   State it clearly—usually as a question.

- **GATHER INFORMATION**   Research; ask questions. Discover what is already known about the problem.

- **STATE A HYPOTHESIS**   A **hypothesis** [hy-PAHTH-uh-sis] is a suggested solution as to why something happens.

- **TEST THE HYPOTHESIS**   Experiment and examine the situation to check the hypothesis.

- **MAKE CAREFUL OBSERVATIONS**   Note everything your senses can gather. Record the **data** [DAYT-uh]. Keep careful records.

- **ORGANIZE AND ANALYZE THE DATA**   Put the data in order. Scientists often use charts and tables to organize data. Figure out the <u>meaning</u> of the data.

- **STATE A CONCLUSION**   Explain the data. State whether or not it supports the hypothesis.

Different problems require different approaches. Not every step in scientific method needs to be used. And the steps can be used in any order.

CHOOSE THE RIGHT CAPTION

Below are eight figures and eight captions. Each caption matches one of the figures. Choose the caption that best describes each figure. Write the correct caption on the line provided.

Choose from these captions:

Identify the problem   Make careful observations

Gather information   Record the data

State a hypothesis   Analyze the data

Test the hypothesis   State a conclusion

Figure A

1. _____

Figure C

3. _____

Figure B

2. _____

Figure D

4. _____

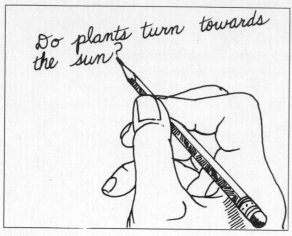

Figure E

5. _____

Figure F

6. _____

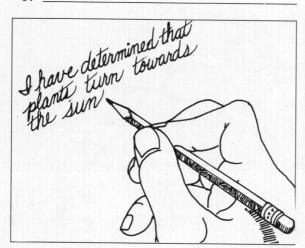

Figure G

7. _____

Figure H

8. _____

MATCHING

Match each term in Column A with its description in Column B. Write the correct letter in the space provided.

Column A	Column B
_____ **1.** analyze	**a)** explains the data
_____ **2.** scientific method	**b)** suggested solution
_____ **3.** conclusion	**c)** test the hypothesis
_____ **4.** hypothesis	**d)** guide for solving problems
_____ **5.** experiment	**e)** figure out the meaning

12

USING YOUR IMAGINATION AND SCIENTIFIC REASONING

Two separate stories are shown in the figures below. However, the figures in each are not in the proper order (sequence). In the table under each set of figures, list the figures in their proper order. Also, explain what is happening in each figure. Finally, write a hypothesis (in question form) and a conclusion.

Figure I

Figure J

Figure K

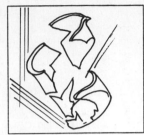

Figure L

Step	Figure	Explanation
1.		
2.		
3.		
4.		

Hypothesis: _____

Conclusion: _____

Figure M

Figure N

Figure O

Figure P

Step	Figure	Explanation
1.		
2.		
3.		
4.		

Hypothesis: _____

Conclusion: _____

FILL IN THE BLANK

Complete each statement using a term or terms from the list below. Write your answers in the spaces provided.

supports	observe	different
problems	question	already known
data	scientific method	senses
steps		

1. To test a hypothesis, scientists may _____ natural events.

2. When scientists research, they may find out what is _____ about a problem.

3. Your _____ gather information.

4. A conclusion states whether or not data _____ a hypothesis.

5. A problem is usually stated as a _____.

6. Scientists use certain _____ to solve problems.

7. You solve _____ much like scientists do.

8. Different problems can be solved in _____ ways.

9. A guide used to solve problems is called _____.

10. Scientists use charts to put _____ in order.

REACHING OUT

Jennifer has never eaten asparagus. She is afraid that it might make her sick. At dinner, she eats some. She likes the taste, but soon she suffers from nausea. Jennifer concludes that asparagus makes her sick.

1. Why might Jennifer's conclusion be <u>incorrect</u>? _____

_____

_____

2. What might be done to further test her conclusion? _____

_____

_____

How are experiments done safely?

caustic: able to burn and irritate the skin
safety alert symbols: signs that warn of hazards or dangers

LESSON 3 | How are experiments done safely?

"Hands-on" experiences are part of many school activities. Science, especially, is suited to "learning by doing." <u>You</u> investigate; <u>you</u> make things happen; <u>you</u> learn from what <u>you</u> do.

Science investigations can be exciting. However, they can also be <u>dangerous</u>. Science laboratories have equipment and materials that can be dangerous if not handled properly. For this reason, it is important for you to always follow proper safety guidelines. Safety rules are for your own protection-as well as the protection of everyone around you.

The safety rules that you should follow are listed on page 17. Read over these safety rules carefully. Notice the **safety alert symbols** that accompany the safety rules. In this book, safety alert symbols are included at the beginning of some activities to make you aware of safety precautions. Always note any safety symbols and caution statements in an activity.

To avoid accidents in the science laboratory, always follow your teacher's directions. You should not perform activities without directions from your teacher. You also should never work in the science laboratory alone.

One hazard has no symbol even though it probably causes more accidents than any others. That hazard is "horsing around." Horsing around in the laboratory can lend to serious injury—or even death. So THINK before doing anything foolish.

CLOTHING PROTECTION • A lab coat protects clothing from stains. • Always confine loose clothing.

 EYE SAFETY • Always wear safety goggles. • If anything gets in your eyes, flush them with plenty of water. • Be sure you know how to use the emergency wash system in the laboratory.

 FIRE SAFETY • Never get closer to an open flame than is necessary. • Never reach across an open flame. • Confine loose clothing. • Tie back loose hair. • Know the location of the fire-extinguisher and fire blanket. • Turn off gas valves when not in use. • Use proper procedures when lighting any burner.

 POISON • Never touch, taste, or smell any unknown substance. Wait for your teacher's instruction.

 CAUSTIC SUBSTANCES • Some chemicals can irritate and burn the skin. If a chemical spills on your skin, flush it with plenty of water. Notify your teacher without delay.

 HEATING SAFETY • Handle hot objects with tongs or insulated gloves. • Put hot objects on a special lab surface or on a heat-resistant pad; never directly on a desk or table top.

 SHARP OBJECTS • Handle sharp objects carefully. • Never point a sharp object at yourself-or anyone else. • Cut in the direction away from your body.

 TOXIC VAPORS • Some vapors (gases) can injure the skin, eyes, and lungs. Never inhale vapors directly. • Use your hand to "wave" a small amount of vapor towards your nose.

 GLASSWARE SAFETY • Never use broken or chipped glassware. • Never pick up broken glass with your bare hands.

 CLEAN UP • Wash your hands thoroughly after any laboratory activity.

 ELECTRICAL SAFETY • Never use an electrical appliance near water or on a wet surface. • Do not use wires if the wire covering seems worn. • Never handle electrical equipment with wet hands.

 DISPOSAL • Discard all materials properly according to your teacher's directions.

PUTTING SAFETY RULES TO USE

Answer the following questions in complete sentences.

1. Jean has long hair. What should she do before working near an open flame. _____

   _____

2. A glass tube has broken. How should you pick up the pieces. _____

   _____

3. Why should you always wear safety goggles during <u>every</u> lab activity?_____

   _____

4. What else should you wear? Why? _____

   _____

5. A chemical spills on your hand. You are pretty sure that it is harmless. But you are

   not certain. What should you do? _____

IDENTIFYING SAFETY ALERT SYMBOLS

Six safety alert symbols are shown below. Match them with their meanings. Write the correct <u>letter</u> next to each description.

a.   b.   c.   d.   e.   f.

_____ 1. electrical safety   _____ 4. clothing protection

_____ 2. fire safety   _____ 5. sharp objects

_____ 3. heating safety   _____ 6. glassware safety

REACHING OUT

In the box at the right, design a NO HORSING AROUND symbol. Either draw it or describe it, or both. Perhaps you can think up more than one.

What are the parts of the earth?

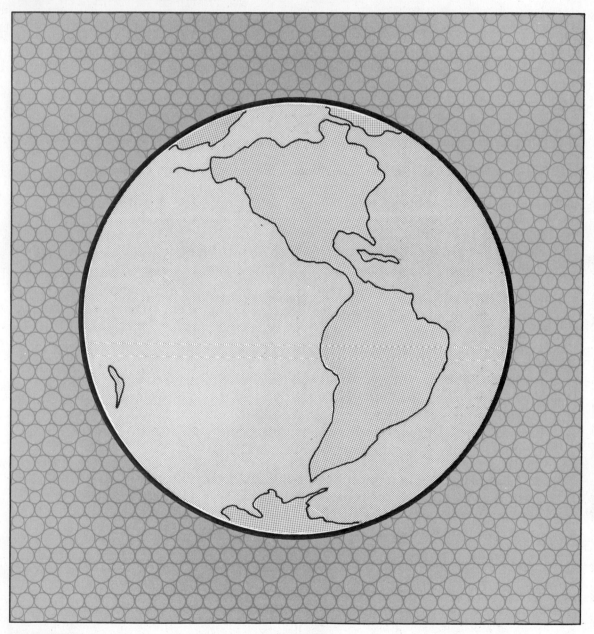

atmosphere [AT-muhs-feer]: layer of gases that surrounds the earth
hydrosphere [HY-droh-sfeer]: part of the earth that is water
lithosphere [LITH-oh-sfeer]: solid part of the earth

LESSON 4 | What are the parts of the earth?

You gaze into the sky on a clear night. What do you see? Stars. The blackness of space is dotted with stars.

Can you see any stars during the daytime? Yes, just one... the sun. The sun is a star. Nine planets circle the sun. We live on one of these planets, the planet Earth

What makes the planet earth so special? Earth has the right conditions for life. It has the proper mixture of gases, reasonable temperature, and a large amount of water. Earth also has solid land that can support life.

Scientists have given names to the solid, liquid and gas parts of the earth. They are the **lithosphere** [LITH-oh-sfeer], the **hydrosphere** [HY-droh-sfeer], and the **atmosphere** [AT-muhs-feer].

LITHOSPHERE The lithosphere is the solid part of the earth. It is made up of rocks, minerals, and soil. The ground you walk on is part of the lithosphere. Mountains also are part of the lithosphere. The lithosphere extends under the oceans and makes up the continents.

HYDROSPHERE The hydrosphere is the part of the earth that is water. Salt water makes up about 97% of the hydrosphere. Salt water is found mostly in the oceans. Fresh water makes up the remaining water on the earth. Fresh water is found in rivers, lakes, and streams. Most of the fresh water of the earth is frozen in glaciers.

ATMOSPHERE The atmosphere is the gas layer that surrounds the earth. The air you breathe is part of the atmosphere. Living things need two important gases of the atmosphere in order to survive. These gases are oxygen and carbon dioxide.

PLANET EARTH

Look at the drawings of the earth. Then follow the directions.

Figure A   **Figure B**

1. Fill in the lithosphere with a pencil
2. Fill in the hydrosphere with a blue pencil or pen.

COMPLETE THE CHART

Complete the chart by filling in the missing information. Place a check mark in the correct column.

	PART	LITHOSPHERE	ATMOSPHERE	HYDROSPHERE
1.	Mountains			
2.	Carbon Dioxide			
3.	Glaciers			
4.	Rivers			
5.	Continents			
6.	Oxygen			
7.	Oceans			
8.	Rocks			
9.	Lakes			
10.	Minerals			

FILL IN THE BLANK

Complete each statement using a term or terms from the list below. Write your answers in the spaces provided.

carbon dioxide	nine	atmosphere
hydrosphere	lithosphere	planet
glaciers	oxygen	temperature
sun	oceans	

1. Earth is a _____ .

2. The planets circle the _____ .

3. _____ planets move around the sun.

4. The solid part of the earth's surface is called the _____ .

5. The gases that surround our planet make up the _____ .

6. The part of the earth that is water is the _____ .

7. Most of the fresh water of the earth is frozen in _____ .

8. Two important gases of the atmosphere are _____ and

   _____ .

9. Life exists on the earth because it has the proper mix of gases, reasonable

   _____ , and a large amount of water.

10. Salt water is found mostly in the _____ .

MATCHING

Match each term in Column A with its description in Column B. Write the correct letter in the space provided.

	Column A		Column B
_____	1. salt water	a)	makes up about 97% of the hydrosphere
_____	2. atmosphere	b)	water layer
_____	3. hydrosphere	c)	rocks, minerals, and soil
_____	4. lithosphere	d)	gases needed by living things
_____	5. oxygen and carbon dioxide	e)	mixture of gases

NAME THE "SPHERES"

Each part of the diagram below belongs to either the atmosphere, the hydrosphere, or the lithosphere.
Find each letter in the diagram. In the space provided, answer the questions.

Figure C

1. Letter A is part of which "sphere"? _____

2. Letter B is part of the _____

3. Letter C is part of the _____

4. Letter D is part of the _____

5. Letter E is part of the _____

TRUE OR FALSE

In the space provided, write "true" if the sentence is true. Write "false" if the sentence is false.

_____ 1. The lithosphere is found only under the oceans.

_____ 2. The lithosphere is a mixture of gases.

_____ 3. Soil is part of the lithosphere.

_____ 4. Oxygen is part of the atmosphere.

_____ 5. Living things need carbon dioxide and oxygen.

_____ 6. The air you breathe is part of the hydrosphere.

_____ 7. Earth has the right conditions for life.

_____ 8. The hydrosphere is made up of a mixture of gases.

_____ 9. Rivers, lakes and oceans are places where salt water is found.

_____ 10. The ground you walk on is part of the lithosphere.

REACHING OUT

Prefixes are word parts that are placed at the beginning of words. Two prefixes are used in this lesson, "litho-" and "hydro". Use a dictionary to find the meanings of these prefixes. Write the meanings of these prefixes below. Then, using the dictionary, find two additional words that contain each prefix. Write these words and their meanings.

"litho-" _____

"hydro-" _____

_____

_____

_____

_____

What is inside the earth?

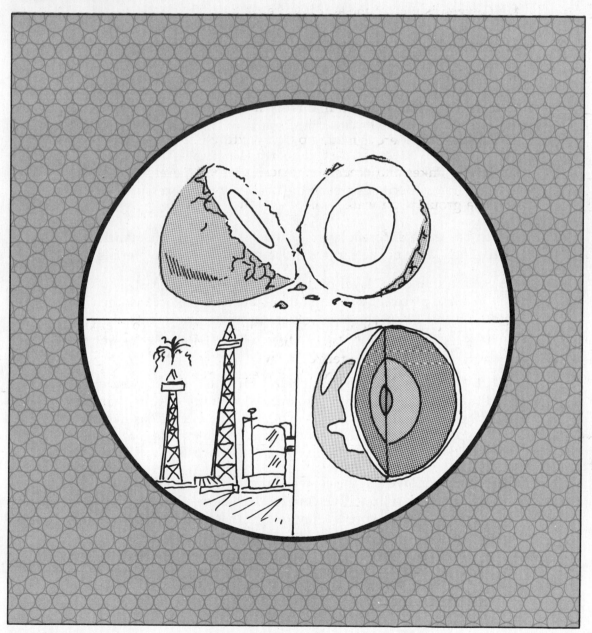

core: inner layer, or center of the earth
crust: thin outer layer of the earth
mantle: thick layer of rock below the crust and above the core

LESSON 5 | What is inside the earth?

If you could dig a hole all the way to the center of the earth, what would you see? Would the earth look the same all the way through?

Scientists have wondered about the inside of the earth. They have found ways to study it. They use special tools to dig out samples from deep inside. Special instruments "look into" parts of the earth we cannot see.

The scientists have learned that the earth is not the same all the way through. The materials are different, so are the temperature and pressure. Temperature becomes greater the deeper you go. Pressure becomes greater too.

The earth has three different layers. They are the **crust**, the **mantle**, and the **core**. Each layer of the earth is made up of different materials.

CRUST   The thin outer layer of the earth is called the crust. The crust is thick in some places and thin in others. Beneath the oceans, the crust is between 5 and 10 km thick. However, under the continents, the crust is between 32 and 70 km thick. The crust is made up of loose rocks and soil. Under the rocks and soil, the crust is solid rock. We live on the crust.

MANTLE   The layer of earth found below the crust, and above the core, is called the mantle. The mantle is about 2900 km thick. More than two-thirds of the mass of the earth is in the mantle. The mantle has two parts. The upper part is solid rock. The lower part of the mantle can flow like a thick liquid. It has the consistency of silly putty.

CORE   The inner layer, or the center of the earth is called the core. The core is about 3500 km thick. The core has two parts, the outer core and the inner core. The <u>outer core</u> is a <u>liquid</u> layer that is about 2200 km thick. It contains melted iron and nickel. The <u>inner core</u> is about 1300 km thick. The inner core is not liquid as many people think. The inner core is made up of <u>solid</u> iron and nickel.

THE EARTH'S LAYERS

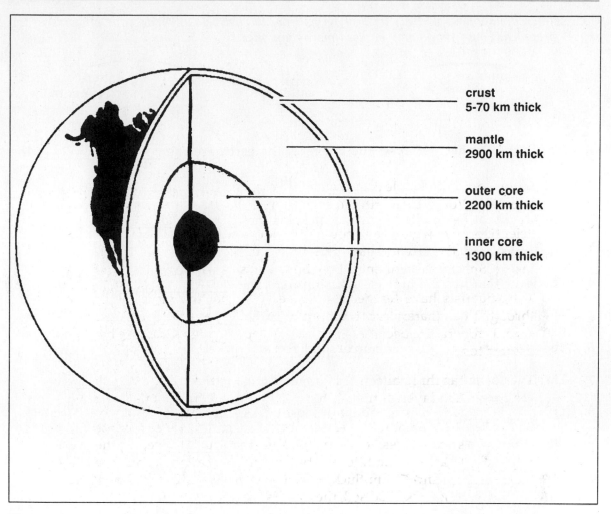

crust
5-70 km thick

mantle
2900 km thick

outer core
2200 km thick

inner core
1300 km thick

Figure A

1. Which layer is the thickest? _____

2. Which layer is the thinnest? _____

3. On which layer do we live? _____

4. Which layer is the hottest? _____

5. Which layer is the coolest? _____

6. Which layer touches the atmosphere? _____

7. Which layer is made up of melted iron and nickel? _____

8. What is the center layer called? _____

9. Name the layer between the crust and the outer core? _____

10. Name the layer between the inner core and the mantle? _____

FILL IN THE BLANK

Complete each statement using a term or terms from the list below. Write your answers in the spaces provided. Some words may be used more than once.

mantle	crust	inner core
upper	outer core	continents
lower		

1. Starting with the top layer, the layers of the earth are the _____ , the _____ , the _____ and the _____ .

2. The layer that has melted iron and nickel is the _____ .

3. The thickest crust is found below the _____ .

4. The layer that has the highest temperature is the _____ .

5. The layer that has the lowest temperature is the _____ .

6. The _____ is made up of solid iron and nickel.

7. The layer of the earth between the core and crust is the _____ .

8. The _____ is made up of loose rocks and soil.

9. More than two-thirds of the earth's mass is in the _____ .

10. The _____ part of the mantle can flow like a thick liquid.

TRUE AND FALSE

In the space provided, write "true" if the sentence is true. Write "false" if the sentence is false.

_____ 1. Every layer of the earth is the same thickness.

_____ 2. The mantle contains soil.

_____ 3. The mantle is the thickest layer.

_____ 4. We live on the crust.

_____ 5. The deeper we go into the earth, the cooler it becomes.

_____ 6. Most of our planet is made of soil.

_____ 7. The lower part of the atmosphere touches the crust.

_____ 8. Pressure is greatest in the inner core.

MODELING THE LAYERS OF THE EARTH

What you need (Materials)

hard-boiled egg   knife

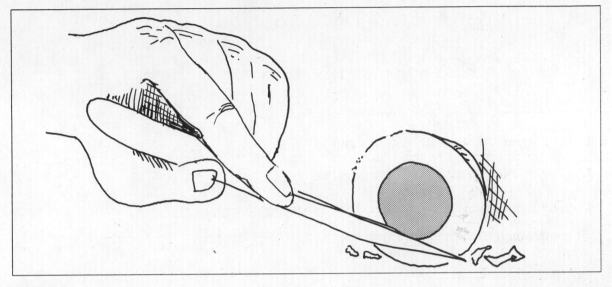

Figure B

How To Do The Experiment (Procedure)

1.   Obtain a hard-boiled egg with the shell on it.

2.   Use the knife to cut the hard-boiled egg in half.

3.   Observe the parts of the egg.

What You Learned (Observations)

1.   Which part of the egg can be compared to the earth's crust? _____.

2.   Which part of the egg can be compared to the earth's mantle? _____.

3.   Which part of the egg can be compared to the earth's core? _____.

Something To Think About (Conclusion)

How do the thicknesses of the layers of the egg compare to the layers of the earth?

_____

_____

_____

MATCHING

Match each term in Column A with its description in column B. Write the correct letter in the space provided.

	Column A		Column B
_____	1. mantle	a)	we live on this layer
_____	2. crust	b)	layer below the crust
_____	3. inner core	c)	contains melted iron and nickel
_____	4. outer core	d)	layer of air
_____	5. atmosphere	e)	contains solid iron and nickel

WORD SCRAMBLE

Below are several scrambled words you have used in this Lesson. Unscramble the words and write your answers in the spaces provided.

1. TELNAM   _____

2. STRUC   _____

3. KILNEC   _____

4. SEPREURS   _____

5. LOSI   _____

REACHING OUT

Scientists believe that our planet was once all melted material. While melted, the different materials separated into layers. How would this explain the fact that the lightest rocks are found in the crust, and heavier materials are found deeper down.

Hint: Throw a penny and a piece of wood into a bowl of water. Watch what happens and think about it.

_____

_____

_____

What makes up the earth's surface?

6

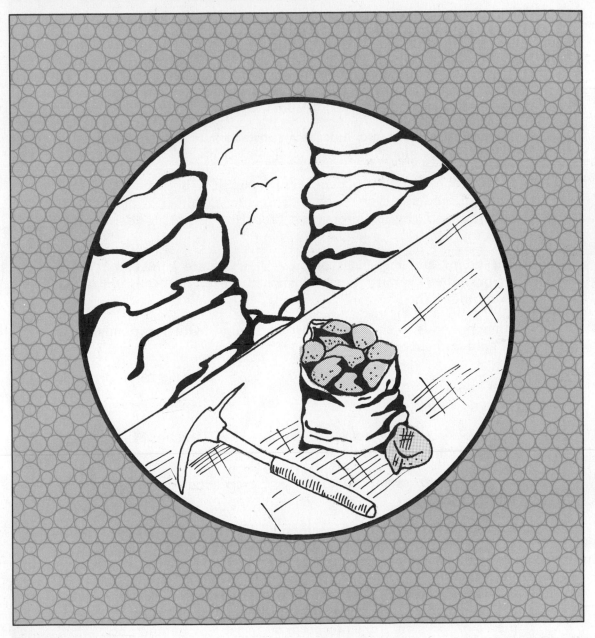

crystal: natural solid substance that has a definite shape
minerals: natural solids formed from elements and compounds in the earth's crust
rock: natural solid that is made up of mineral grains stuck together

LESSON 6 | What makes up the earth's surface?

Many people collect rocks and minerals. They are found almost everywhere. Did you ever pick up an interesting rock and study it?

Rocks and minerals are closely related, but they are not the same. How are they the same? How are they different?

MINERALS

- **Minerals** are natural solids formed from elements and compounds in the earth's crust. They are not laboratory made.

- Minerals are inorganic. Inorganic substances do not contain matter that was once alive.

- A mineral has a definite chemical make-up. It is the same all the way through, and it never changes. Therefore, <u>a mineral has definite chemical and physical properties</u>. Properties help us to identify different minerals.

- The atoms and molecules of most minerals are joined in regular shapes called crystals. A crystal is a natural solid substance that has a definite shape.

- Some minerals, such as quartz are compounds. Other minerals, such as gold and silver are elements.

ROCKS

- **Rocks**, like minerals, are solid

- Some rocks contain matter that was once alive. Coal, for example was formed from dead plant matter.

- Most rocks are made up of mineral grains that have been stuck together.

- A rock has no definite composition. One part may be different from another part. Therefore, a rock has no definite properties. <u>Rocks cannot be grouped by properties.</u>

- Rocks are grouped by the way they were formed. Rocks are formed in three ways; (1) when melted minerals cool and harden; (2) when pieces of rocks and minerals become cemented together, and; (3) when existing rocks are slowly changed by heat and pressure.

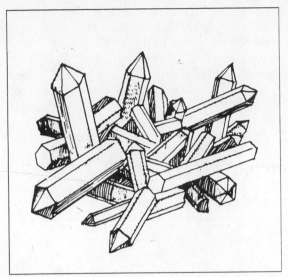

Figure A *Quartz*

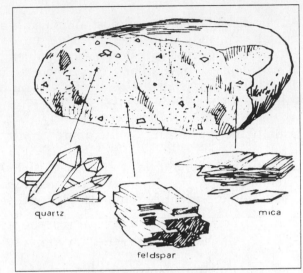

Figure B *Granite*

Quartz is a common mineral.

Quartz comes in many colors and sizes... but its natural shape is always the same.

The natural shape of most minerals is called its crystal form. The shape of a mineral's crystals helps us identify the mineral.

Use Figure A to answer the following.

1. How many sides does the mineral quartz have? _____

2. Does a quartz crystal always have this many sides?_____

3. What do we call the natural shape of a mineral? _____

Quartz also is known as silicon dioxide. Quartz is made up of silicon and oxygen.

4. Does the chemical makeup of quartz ever change _____

5. Is every part of quartz the same? _____

Granite is common rock. Granite is a mixture of minerals quartz, feldspar, and at least one other material, such as mica, or hornblende.

Use Figure B to answer the following

6. Is every part of granite the same? _____

7. Does granite have a definite chemical makeup? _____

As you already learned, almost all minerals are made up of tiny crystals. The atoms in a crystal are arranged in a certain pattern to form the shape. This pattern is repeated over and over. The crystals that make up a mineral always have the same shape, but may differ in size. For example, quartz crystals are hexagonal (six-sided). If you have a large piece of quartz, the crystals are hexagonal. If you have a small piece of quartz, the crystals are still hexagonal.

Usually the crystals of a mineral are very small. Large, single crystals are rare.

Each kind of mineral has a specific crystal shape. There are six basic shapes of crystals. Scientists use X-rays to study the structure of a crystal. They can use the structure of the crystal to help identify minerals. Figure C shows the six basic crystal shapes.

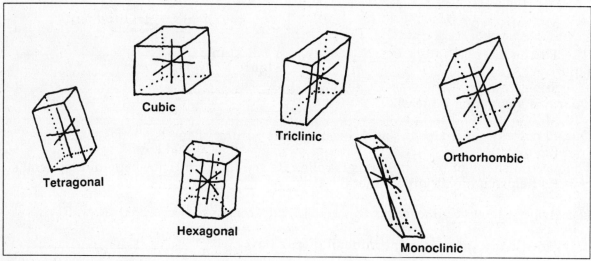

Figure C *The Six Basic Crystals Shapes.*

Using Figure C and the following information answer the following questions.

1. What are crystals? _____

2. What are the six main crystal shapes? _____

_____

3. Why is it important to know the shape of a mineral's crystals? _____

_____

4. How do you think the cubic crystal shape got its name? _____

_____

5. What do scientists use to study crystal structure?—_____

FILL IN THE BLANK

Complete each statement using a term or terms from the list below. Write your answers in the spaces provided. Some words may be used more than once.

six	do not	does
minerals	found in nature	formed
alive	crystal	properties

1. Minerals are always _____ .

2. Rocks _____ have definite _____ .

3. A mineral _____ have a definite chemical make-up.

4. Minerals have definite _____ that help us identify them.

5. There are _____ basic crystal forms.

6. Rocks contain matter that was once _____ .

7. Most rocks are mixtures of two or more _____ .

8. Rocks _____ have a definite chemical make-up.

9. Rocks are grouped by how they were _____ .

10. A _____ is a natural solid that has a definite shape.

MATCHING

Match each term in Column A with its description in Column B. Write the correct letter in the space provided.

	Column A		Column B
_____	1. mineral	a)	help us identify substances
_____	2. rock	b)	a rock
_____	3. properties	c)	definite chemical make-up
_____	4. a mixture of two or more minerals	d)	made up of rocks and minerals
_____	5. earth's crust	e)	grouped by how its formed

TRUE OR FALSE

In the space provided, Write "true" if the sentence is true. Write "false" if the sentence is false.

_____ **1.** The earth's crust is made up only of rocks.

_____ **2.** Minerals are made from rocks.

_____ **3.** Every part of a mineral is the same.

_____ **4.** Every part of a rock is the same.

_____ **5.** A mineral has a definite chemical make-up.

_____ **6.** A rock has a definite chemical make-up.

_____ **7.** Gold and silver are compounds.

_____ **8.** Quartz has hexagonal crystals.

_____ **9.** Minerals contain material from dead plants and animals.

_____ **10.** Rocks are grouped according to size.

MINERAL OR ROCK?

Complete the chart by putting a check mark, (✓) in the correct box.

	MINERAL	ROCK
1. definite chemical make-up		
2. no definite chemical make-up		
3. made of matter that was never alive		
4. sometimes has matter that was once alive		
5. properties always the same		
6. mixture of minerals		
7. diamond		
8. granite		
9. quartz		
10. talc		

What are minerals?

7

abrasive [uh-BRAY-siv]:   an item used for scraping or rubbing
ore: mineral that is mined because it contains useful metals or nonmetals

LESSON 7 | What are minerals?

Many minerals are beautiful. Diamonds, sapphires, rubies, and emeralds are beautiful—and expensive. They are often worn as jewelry. So are other, less precious, minerals.

Minerals—even diamonds—have practical uses too. Here are a few examples.

CUTTING AND GRINDING   Diamonds are the hardest minerals. Diamonds are important in industry. They are used for cutting and grinding.

ABRASIVES   Things used for rubbing are called **abrasives** [uh-BRAY-sivz]. Aluminum oxide and quartz are two minerals used as abrasives.

Very <u>fine</u> abrasives, such as emery paper, are used for <u>polishing</u>. <u>Medium</u> abrasives, such as scouring powder, are used for <u>removing</u> dirt. <u>Rough</u> abrasives, such as sandpaper, are used to <u>rub</u> <u>off</u> thicker and harder surfaces like wood and paint.

GLASS-MAKING   Quartz is used in making some types of glass.

PLASTER   Gypsum [JIP-sum] is used in plaster of Paris, an important building material.

ENERGY   Uranium is supplying more and more of our energy. Uranium supplies atomic energy.

METAL PRODUCTS   Most metals come from minerals. We need metals for cooking, building, and many other uses. A mineral that is mined because it contains useful metals or nonmetals is an **ore**.

FARMING   Mineral fertilizers help farmers grow bigger, healthier food crops.

People use great amounts of minerals. We must not waste them. We must learn ways to reuse minerals and to use them wisely. Nature is not putting back what people have taken out.

USES OF MINERALS

Many products are made from minerals. Gypsum is used to make plaster of Paris. Quartzite is used to make glass, sandpaper and various electronic equipment. Diamonds are used to make jewelry. Diamonds are so hard that they also are used to make cutting and drilling tools.

Some kinds of minerals are needed by humans to keep the body in good health. Calcium and phosphorus are two minerals the body need for strong bones and teeth. Iron is a mineral used by the body to make red blood cells.

Figure A

Figure B

Some minerals are rare and expensive. These minerals are called gems. Diamonds, rubies, and emeralds are examples of gems.

1. What are these minerals used for? _____

2. Are the shapes shown in Figure A the mineral's natural shape? _____

   Gold and silver also are minerals.

3. Gold and silver are _____.
   _{elements, compounds}

   The mineral talc has many uses. It is used to make soap, crayons, and talcum powder.

4. Talc is a _____ mineral.
   _{hard, soft}

Figure C

Figure D

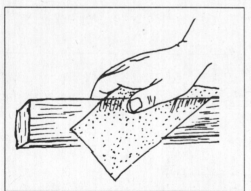

Figure E

Figure F

Some drill bits are tipped with diamond.

1. Diamond is _____ than rock.
   <small>harder, softer</small>

2. Diamond is _____ than steel.
   <small>harder, softer</small>

3. What would you use to clean this pot?

   _____

4. Which minerals might this product have?

   _____ or _____

5. Which mineral is used for most sandpaper?

   _____

6. Which mineral is found in plaster of Paris?

   _____

FILL IN THE BLANK

Complete each statement using a term or terms from the list below. Write your answers in the spaces provided. Some words may be used more than once.

aluminum oxide	jewelery	hard
iron	rough	soft
quartz	ores	gypsum

1. An abrasive feels _____.

2. The mineral most often used as an abrasive is _____.

3. Diamonds are used in industry because they are so _____.

4. Precious minerals are used mostly as _____.

5. Some glass contains _____.

6. Plaster of Paris contains the mineral _____.

7. Scouring powder contains either quartz or _____.

8. Minerals that give us useful metals or nonmetals are called _____.

9. Talc is a _____ mineral.

10. The mineral used by the body to produce red blood cells is _____.

MATCHING

Match each term in Column A with its description in Column B. Write the correct letter in the space provided.

	Column A		Column B
_____ 1.	abrasives	a)	contain useful metals or nonmetals
_____ 2.	ores	b)	a precious gem
_____ 3.	quartz	c)	needed for strong bones and teeth
_____ 4.	sapphire	d)	used to make some types of glass
_____ 5.	calcium and phosphorus	e)	rough

TRUE OR FALSE

In the space provided, write "true" if the sentence is true. Write "false" if the sentence is false.

_____ 1. Diamonds are used only as jewelry.

_____ 2. An abrasive is rough.

_____ 3. Diamonds are good for grinding and cutting.

_____ 4. Gypsum is an important part of glass.

_____ 5. Every mineral is an ore.

_____ 6. There is only one kind of ore.

_____ 7. Metals come from ores.

_____ 8. Diamond is harder than steel.

_____ 9. Talc is used as an abrasive.

_____ 10. Diamond is important in industry.

WORD SCRAMBLE

Below are several scrambled words you have used in this Lesson. Unscramble the words and write your answers in the spaces.

1. BRAVESAI   _____

2. MADNOID   _____

3. ROE   _____

4. SGALS   _____

5. UPSMYG   _____

REACHING OUT

What steps should we take to keep our supplies of minerals from running out?

_____

_____

_____

What properties are used to identify minerals?

8

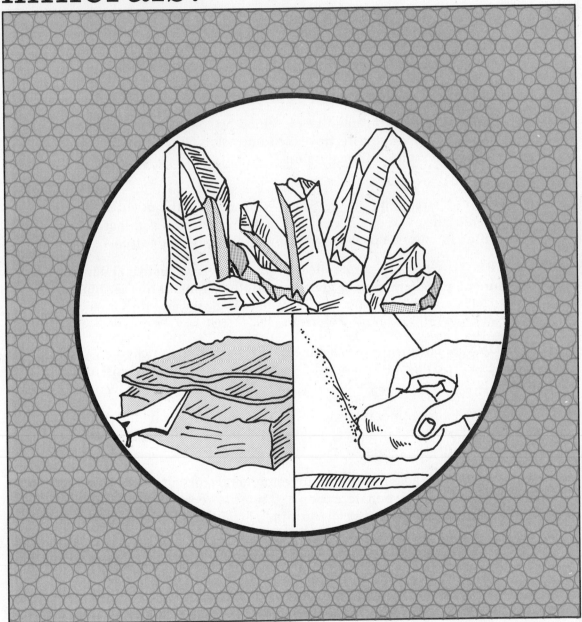

cleavage [KLEE-vij]:   splitting of a mineral into pieces with smooth, flat surfaces
density [DEN-suh-tee]:   amount of matter in a given volume
fracture [FRACK-chur]:   splitting of a mineral into pieces with uneven surfaces
hardness: property of a mineral to resist being scratched
luster: way a mineral reflects light from its surface
streak: color of the powder left by a mineral

LESSON 8 | What properties are used to identify minerals

Have you ever heard of "fool's gold?" It looks like gold, but it is another mineral. It is worth far less than gold. Many people have been fooled by it.

Many minerals have "look-alikes." That is why scientists have come up with different properties and tests to identify minerals. Sometimes, a mineral can be identified by only one property. However, usually several properties must be tested in order to identify the mineral.

The properties of minerals are:

COLOR Most minerals cannot be identified by color alone. Many minerals, such as gold and pyrite, have the same color. Other minerals, such as quartz, have many different colors.

STREAK When you rub a mineral on a piece of unglazed ceramic tile, it may leave a **streak** of powder. Streak is the color of the powder left by the mineral. The color of a mineral's streak is important. A mineral may have different colors, but it <u>always</u> leaves the same color streak.

LUSTER The way a mineral reflects light is called its **luster**. The luster of a mineral is either shiny or glassy and dull. A mineral that is <u>shiny</u> is said to have a <u>metallic</u> luster. A mineral that is <u>glassy</u> <u>and</u> <u>dull</u> is said to have a <u>nonmetallic</u> luster.

HARDNESS The property of a mineral to resist being scratched is called **hardness**. To find out how hard a mineral is, we test it against other minerals.

DENSITY Every mineral has its own **density** [DEN-sih-tee]. Density is the amount of matter in a given volume. For this reason, density often is used to identify minerals.

ACID TEST The acid test is used to test minerals for calcium carbonate. To test for calcium carbonate, a drop of dilute hydrochloric acid is placed on the mineral. If bubbles form, the mineral contains calcium carbonate.

CRYSTAL SHAPE As you learned in Lesson 6, each mineral has a specific shape. Crystal shape can help identify some minerals.

FRACTURE AND CLEAVAGE The way a mineral splits can also be used to identify the mineral. Some minerals split into smooth, flat pieces. These minerals are said to have **cleavage** [KLEE-vij]. Other minerals split into pieces with uneven surfaces. These minerals are said to have **fracture** [FRAK-chur].

HARDNESS The Moh's scale of Hardness shows the ten minerals that we test other materials against. When a material is tested for hardness, it is given a number to show how hard it is. A material with a hardness of 2.5 would be harder than gypsum, but softer than calcite. A mineral can scratch something softer, but not something harder.

	Hardness		Mineral
Softest	1.		talc
	2.		gypsum
	3.		calcite
	4.		flourite
	5.		apatite
	6.		feldspar
	7.		quartz
	8.		topaz
	9.		corundum
Hardest	10.		diamond

1. Which mineral cannot scratch any mineral by itself?

_____

2. Which is harder, calcite or topaz?

_____

3. Copper can scratch talc and gypsum, but it cannot scratch fluorite. What is its hardness?

_____

4. Graphite has a hardness of 1.5. What mineral could graphite scratch?

_____

5. Quartz has a hardness of 7.5-8. Name two minerals that can easily scratch quartz.

_____

DENSITY All matter has mass and volume. Matter also has density. Every mineral has its own density. Therefore density can be used to help identify minerals.

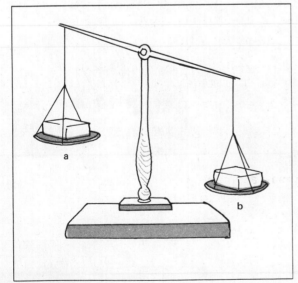

Figure A

Study diagram A and answer these questions.

6. Which weighs more, mineral a or b?

_____

7. The chunks of minerals a and b are

of _____ sizes.
    the same, different

8. Mineral b is _____
                        more, less
dense than mineral a.

45

COLOR Most minerals cannot be identified by their color alone. However, there are two minerals that can be identified by their colors, malachite [MAL-uh-kyt] and azurite [AZH-uh-rite]. Malachite is always green. Azurite is always blue.

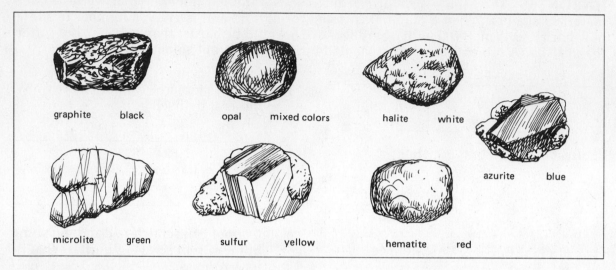

Figure B *Common minerals and their colors.*

LUSTER Luster is divided into two classes, metallic or nonmetalic. Minerals that do not shine like metal have nonmetallic luster.

STREAK Streaking is done by rubbing a mineral on an unglazed ceramic tile. The streak is the color of the mineral's powder. Some minerals leave a clear streak. Some minerals streak the same color as the mineral. Some streak a different color than the mineral.

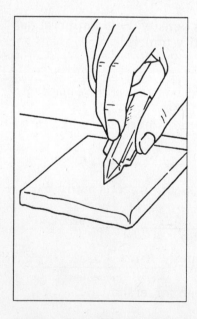

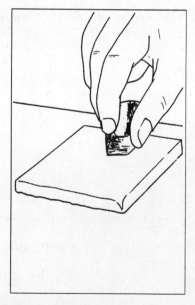

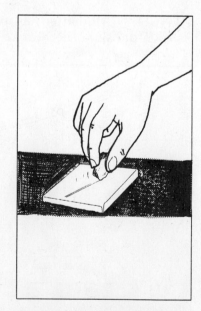

Figure C *The mineral quartz leaves a clear streak.*

Figure D *The mineral iron pyrite is yellow, but it streaks greenish-black.*

Figure E *Gold streaks its own color.*

CLEAVAGE There are many kinds of cleavage. However, the cleavage of a mineral is always the same for that mineral. Cleavage can be used to identify a mineral. Here are three examples of cleavage.

Figure F *Quartz shows no definite cleavage*

Figure G *Calcite cleaves in a very definite pattern.*

Figure H *Mica cleaves easily in thin sheets.*

THE ACID TEST The Acid test is used to test minerals for calcium carbonate ($CaCO_3$). Calcite, dolomite, and malachite are three minerals that contain calcium carbonate.

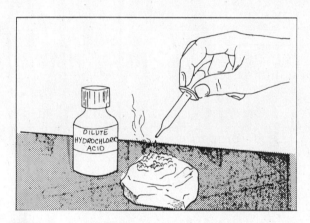

Figure I *Bubbles are given off if calcite is present.*

What acid do you use for the acid test?

_____

What does the acid test tell you about a mineral?

_____

What happens to the surface of a mineral if the acid test is positive?

_____

MATCHING

Match each term in Column A with its description in Column B. Write the correct letter in the space provided.

Column A

_____ 1. streak

_____ 2. cleavage

_____ 3. luster

_____ 4. hardness

_____ 5. crystal

Column B

a) pattern of split minerals

b) property of a mineral to resist being scratched

c) color of a mineral's powder

d) mineral's natural shape

e) way a mineral reflects light

FILL IN THE BLANK

Complete each statement using a term or terms from the list below. Write your answers in the spaces provided.

ten	breaks	share
luster	density	talc
powder	crystal	calcium carbonate
diamond		

1. There are _____ minerals on the hardness scale.

2. The hardest mineral is _____ .

3. The softest mineral is _____ .

4. Metallic and nonmetallic are kinds of _____ .

5. The natural shape of mineral is called its _____ .

6. Cleavage is shown when a mineral _____ .

7. Streak is the color of a mineral's _____ .

8. The weight of a mineral compared to its volume is called its _____ .

9. Dilute hydrochloric acid tests for _____ .

10. Often, several minerals _____ some properties.

TRUE OR FALSE

In the space provided, write "true" if the sentence is true. Write "false" if the sentence is false.

_____ 1. All minerals have the same hardness.

_____ 2. Minerals come in many different colors.

_____ 3. Every mineral has a color.

_____ 4. Every mineral has a crystal form.

_____ 5. A mineral may have a crystal form but no cleavage.

_____ 6. Some minerals leave no streak.

_____ 7. A mineral's streak is always the same color as the mineral.

_____ 8. Hydrochloric acid makes calcium carbonate bubble.

_____ 9. In the Moh's scale, a mineral with a high number can scratch any mineral with a lower number.

_____ 10. All minerals have the same cleavage.

HOW CAN MINERALS TESTED IN CLASS

What You Need (Materials)

quartz   galena   unglazed ceramic tile
pyrite   hematite   medicine dropper
calcite   dilute hydrochloric acid

How To Do The Experiment (Procedure)

1. Examine the samples of quartz, pyrite, calcite, galena, and hematite. What color are they? Record your observations in Table 1.

2. Examine the samples of quartz, pyrite, calcite, galena, and hematite. What kind of luster do they have? Record your observations in Table 1.

3. Rub a piece of quartz along the ceramic tile. What color streak does it leave? Record your observations in Table 1.

4. Repeat Step 3 for the pyrite, calcite, galena, and hematite.

5. Using the medicine dropper, place a few drops of the dilute hydrochloric acid on the quartz. What happens? Record your observations in Table 1.

6. Repeat Step 5 for the pyrite, calcite, galena, and hematite.

What You Learned (Observations)

Table 1

		Quartz	Pyrite	Calcite	Galena	Hematite
1.	Color					
2.	Kind of luster (metallic or nonmetallic)					
3.	Does it streak?					
4.	What color					
5.	Does it react with hydro-chloric acid?					

Something To think About (Conclusions)

1. Why can color alone not be used to identify minerals?

    _____

2. What conclusion can you make about the chemical makeup of calcite based upon its

    reaction to the acid test? _____

WORD SEARCH

The list on the left contains words that you have used in this Lesson. Find and circle each word where it appears in the box. The spellings may go in any direction: up, down, left, right, or diagonally.

QUARTZ

DIAMOND

GYPSUM

DENSITY

CLEAVAGE

STREAK

LUSTER

HARDNESS

ACID

CRYSTAL

Q	T	D	S	L	L	R	A	D	E	C	R	Q
C	U	I	G	U	U	T	R	G	A	U	Y	Y
R	R	A	Z	Y	I	S	A	U	K	N	T	D
Y	A	M	R	R	P	V	T	A	Q	I	I	D
S	N	O	E	T	A	S	E	E	S	R	U	I
T	I	N	A	E	Z	R	U	N	R	M	P	N
A	U	D	L	C	T	G	E	M	P	N	U	A
L	M	C	Y	S	I	D	C	A	I	D	M	O
I	R	A	H	A	R	D	N	E	S	S	S	M

REACHING OUT

Iron pyrite is sometimes known as "fool's gold." If you had a yellow mineral, what would be one test you could use to see if it were real gold or iron pyrite?

_____

_____

50

What are igneous rocks?   9

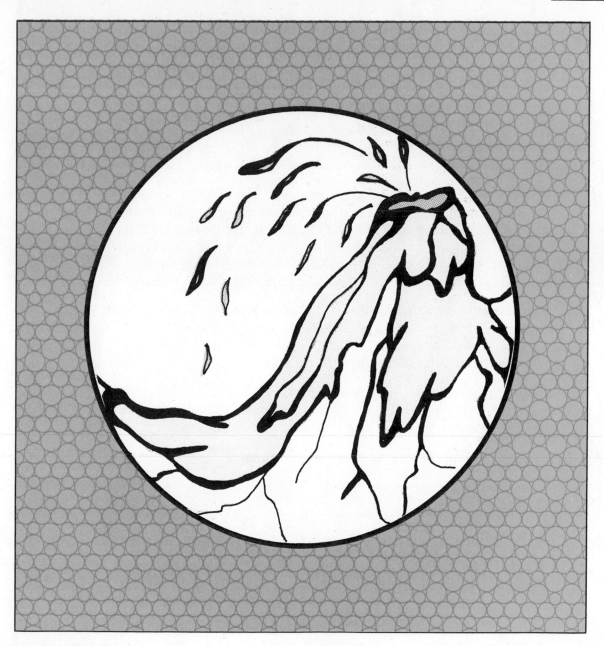

igneous [IG-nee-us] **rocks:**   rocks that form from melted minerals
lava [LAH-vuh]:   magma that reaches the earth's surface
magma [MAG-muh]:   molten rock inside the earth

LESSON 9 | What are igneous rocks?

Do you think it is hot inside the earth? It is very hot. Between the crust and the mantle, the temperature is high enough to melt minerals. So, some of the rock inside the earth is in a liquid state.

What happens if the liquid rock is cooled? **Igneous** [IG-nee-us] **rocks** are formed. Igneous rocks are rocks that form when melted minerals cool and harden. The word "igneous" comes from the Greek word for "fire." Although igneous rocks are not formed by fire, very high temperatures melt rock.

Melted minerals inside the earth are called **magma** [MAG-muh]. There is a lot of magma deep inside the earth. Sometimes, magma rises to the upper part of the earth's crust. The temperature of the crust is much cooler. The magma cools and hardens. Igneous rock is formed. It may take thousands of years for igneous rock to form from magma.

Sometimes, magma forces its way to the surface of the earth. Then it is called **lava** [LAH-vuh]. Lava cools when it has contact with air or water. Cooling makes the lava harden into igneous rock. It does not take a long time for igneous rocks to form from lava.

How can we look at an igneous rock and tell if it cooled slowly or quickly? Igneous rocks have crystals of different sizes. Different speeds of cooling made different size crystals.

- Slow cooling forms rocks with large crystals.

- Rapid cooling forms rocks with small crystals.

- Extra-fast cooling forms rocks with no crystals.

The <u>slower</u> the <u>cooling</u>, the <u>larger</u> the <u>crystals</u>. The <u>faster</u> the <u>cooling</u>, the <u>smaller</u> the <u>crystals</u>.

SOME IGNEOUS ROCKS

Figure A *Granite*

Figure B *Basalt*

Granite is the most common rock on the earth's surface. Granite has large crystals that you can see and feel. Igneous rocks with large crystals also are said to have large grains and a coarse texture. Basalt crystals are very tiny. You need a microscope to see them. Igneous rocks with small crystals have a fine texture.

1. Which igneous rock above has larger crystals?_____

2. This shows that it cooled_____ .
   <small>slowly, quickly</small>

3. Which rock above has small crystals?_____

4. This shows that it cooled_____ .
   <small>slowly, quickly</small>

5. Granite has a_____ texture. Basalt has a_____ texture.
   <small>coarse, fine</small>   <small>coarse, fine</small>

Figure C *Pumice*

Figure D *Obsidian*

Pumice has many holes. But these holes are not crystals. They were made by gases.

Obsidian is called "natural glass."

6. Pumice and obsidian cooled _____ .
   <small>extra fast, extra slow</small>

Study Figure E. Then answer the questions below. You will have to figure out the answers from facts you have learned.

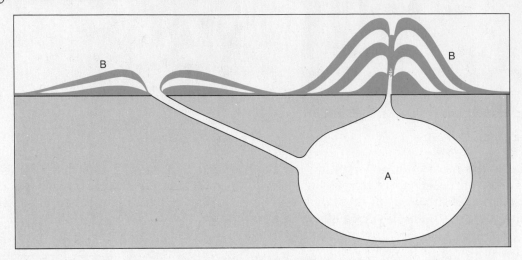

Figure E

This diagram shows two cone-shaped mountains formed by lava. Most people call these mountains <u>volcanoes</u>.

1. Lava is found at _____ .
    _{A, B}

2. Magma is found at _____ .
    _{A, B}

3. Magma cools _____ because it is _____ .
    _{slowly, quickly}   _{under the ground, on the earth's surface}

4. Lava cools _____ because it is _____
    _{slowly, quickly}   _{under the ground, on the earth's surface}

5. Igneous rocks with large crystals form from _____ .
    _{lava, magma}

6. Igneous rocks with small crystals or no crystals at all form from _____
    _{lava , magma}

7. Granite has _____ crystals.
    _{large, small, no}

8. Pumice has _____ crystals.
    _{large, small, no}

9. Granite may form at _____ .
    _{A, B}

10. Pumice may form at _____ .
    _{A, B}

FILL IN THE BLANK

Complete each statement using a term or terms from the list below. Write your answers in the spaces provided. Some words may be used more than once.

large   melted   granite
magma   lava   crystal
small   volcano   slowly

1. Igneous rocks were formed from _____ minerals.

2. Melted rock under the ground is called _____ .

3. Melted rock that comes to the surface is called _____ .

4. Lava may form a mountain called a _____ .

5. An example of an igneous rock formed from magma is _____ .

6. Granite crystals are _____ in size because granite cooled _____ .

7. Grain size is another way of saying _____ size.

8. Basalt crystals are _____ in size.

9. Melted minerals that cool slowly form _____ size crystals.

10. Melted minerals that cool rapidly form _____ size crystals.

MATCHING

Match each term in Column A with its description in Column B. Write the correct letter in the space povided.

Column A	Column B
_____ 1. magma	a) from super-fast cooling
_____ 2. lava	b) from fast cooling
_____ 3. no crystals	c) melted minerals on the surface
_____ 4. large crystals	d) melted minerals below the ground
_____ 5. small crystals	e) from slow cooling

TRUE OR FALSE

In the space provided, write "true" if the sentence is true. Write "false" if the sentence is false.

_____ 1. Magma is solid

_____ 2. Magma contains minerals.

_____ 3. Obsidian is called "natural glass."

_____ 4. Magma is melted rock that has come to the surface.

_____ 5. Lava cools faster than magma.

_____ 6. Granite formed underground.

_____ 7. Granite cooled rapidly.

_____ 8. Granite has small crystals.

_____ 9. Lava rocks usually have large grains.

_____ 10. Fast cooling causes small grains.

_____ 11. Basalt is an igneous rock.

_____ 12. Basalt cooled slowly.

_____ 13. Basalt has small crystals.

_____ 14. Pumice was formed deep underground.

_____ 15. Pumice has no crystals.

REACHING OUT

One of the igneous rocks discussed in this lesson can float on water.

1. Which rock is it? _____

2. Why can it float? _____

What are sedimentary rocks?

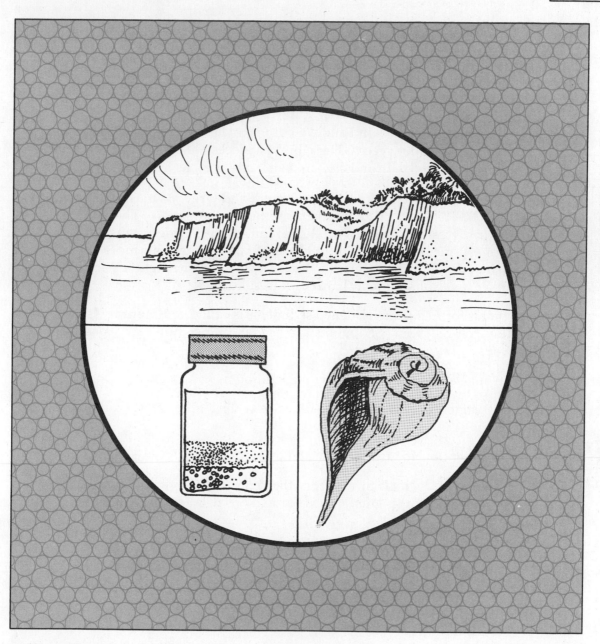

sedimentary [sed-uh-MEN-tuh-ree] **rocks:** rock that forms from pieces of other rocks or the remains of once-living things

LESSON 10 | What are sedimenary rocks?

The tallest mountain in the world is Mount Everest, in Asia. People have risked their lives trying to climb it. But someday, Mount Everest will be completely worn away. It is wearing away right now, a little bit at a time. It will take millions of years for Mount Everest to wear away, but it will happen.

Forces in nature, such as wind and water, keep breaking rocks and soil into smaller and smaller pieces. These broken pieces are called fragments. Pebbles, gravel, sand, silt, and clay are five kinds of rocks fragments.

Fragments are moved about by water, wind, and large ice masses called glaciers [GLAY- shurz]. The fragments settle in a new place. The settled fragments are called sediments [SED-uh-munts]. As time passes, older layers of sediments are buried by new layers. As more and more sediments are added to the layers, the lower layers become tightly packed. The lower layer of sediment hardens into solid rock.

Rock that is formed from hardened sediments is called **sedimentary** [sed-uh-MEN-tuh-ree] **rock**. Sediments can harden into sedimentary rock in two ways:

1. from the pressure of its own weight, or

2. by cementing. Minerals dissolved in water "glue" the sediment together.

Most sediment builds up under water.

Some sedimentary rock forms from the remains of living things, and shells. Soft coal, for example, was formed from layers of dead plant matter.

Some sedimentary rocks also form from minerals dissolved in water. For example, rock salt is a sedimentary rock made up of the mineral halite. Different kinds of sediment form different kinds of sedimentary rocks.

WHAT HAPPENS WHEN WE MIX MUD AND SAND IN WATER?

What You Need (Materials)

mud   jar
sand   stirrer
water cup

Figure A

How To Do the Experiment (Procedure)

1. Fill the jar 3/4 full with water.

2. Add about 1/2 cup of sand and 1/2 cup of mud to the jar.

3. Stir the mixture well.

4. Allow the mixture to stand.

When sediments settle in water, the heaviest sediments settle first. Then the lighter sediments settle.

What You Learned (Observations)

1. What happened to the mud and sand? _____

2. Which sediment settled first? _____

3. The mud settled _____ the sand.
   _{on top of, under}

4. Which sediment is heavier? _____
   _{sand, mud}

Something To Think About (Conclusion)

Pebbles are heavier than sand. If you had added pebbles to your jar, which sediment

would have settled first? _____

EXAMPLES OF SEDIMENTARY ROCKS

Figure B

Shale is a sedimentary rock. It was formed from mud and clay being pressed together.

Shale is very soft rock. It breaks easily.

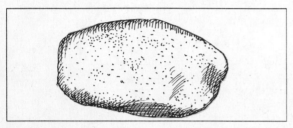

Figure C

Sandstone was formed in water from sand grains. Minerals dissolved in the water cemented the grains together.

Sandstone grains are held together loosely. They can be rubbed off easily.

Figure D

A conglomerate is a sedimentary rock made of gravel and pebbles.

The gravel was cemented together by minerals dissolved in water.

Conglomerate is also called puddingstone.

Figure E

Soft coal is a sedimentary rock.

Soft coal was formed from layers of dead plants.

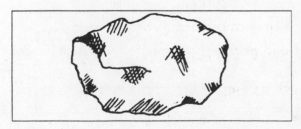

Figure F

Rock salt is a sedimentary rock which formed from the mineral deposits of halite. When water evaporates from salt lakes and shallow seas, the salts are left behind. These salts form halite.

FILL IN THE BLANK

Complete each statement using a term or terms from the list below. Write your answers in the spaces provided.

cementing	moving water	coal
sand	pebbles	sedimentary
fragments	clay	break up
wind	halite	gravel
under water	shale	pressure
silt	glaciers	

1. Forces in nature _____ big rocks into smaller and smaller pieces.

2. Broken pieces of rock are called _____ .

3. Rock that is formed from hardened sediment is called _____ rock.

4. Rock salt is made up of the mineral _____ .

5. Examples of sediments are _____ , _____ , _____ _____ , and _____ .

6. Rock fragments may be moved by _____ , _____ , and _____ .

7. Sediments can harden into sedimentary rocks in two ways. The two ways are from_____ and by _____ .

8. Sedimentary rock made from mud and clay is called _____ .

9. Sedimentary rock made from layers of dead plants is called _____ .

10. Most sedimentary rocks were formed _____ .

MATCHING

Match each term in Column A with its description in Column B. Write the correct letter in the space provided.

Column A	Column B
_____ 1. sedimentary rocks	a) formed from pebbles and gravel
_____ 2. sandstone	b) where most sediment builds up
_____ 3. shale	c) group of rocks formed from sediments
_____ 4. in water	d) formed from mud and clay
_____ 5. conglomerate	e) formed from sand grains

TRUE OR FALSE

In the space provided, write "true" if the sentence is true. Write "false" if the sentence is false.

_____ 1. All rocks are sedimentary rocks.

_____ 2. Different kinds of sediment form different kinds of sedimentary rocks.

_____ 3. Sedimentary rocks are made of rock fragments.

_____ 4. Most sedimentary rocks were formed under water.

_____ 5. All sedimentary rocks were hardened by natural cement.

_____ 6. Rock salt forms from minerals.

_____ 7. Sedimentary rocks can come from other sedimentary rocks.

_____ 8. Sand fragments settle faster than pebbles do.

_____ 9. Rock fragments are carried away by moving water.

_____ 10. Settled fragments of rock are called sediments.

WORD SCRAMBLE

Below are several scrambled words you have used in this Lesson. Unscramble the words and write your answers in the spaces provided.

1. GENTSFRAM _____

2. MESTDINE _____

3. SNOTSEADN _____

4. VAGLER _____

5. HALES _____

What are metamorphic rocks?

metamorphic [met-uh-MOWR-fik] **rock:** rock that forms from pieces of other rocks or the remains of once-living things

LESSON 11 | What are metamorphic rocks?

Many things we use are changed over from what they were to begin with. For example, glass, plastic, and synthetic fabrics do not look like the raw materials they came from. Many of the things we use were changed. Several forces can cause change. Two of these are <u>heat</u> and <u>pressure</u>.

Heat and pressure can change many things. They can even change rocks and the minerals in them. The name for changed-over rocks is **metamorphic** [met-uh-MOWR-fik] **rocks**. Metamorphic comes from Greek words meaning "change" and "form."

Metamorphic rocks are formed deep in the earth where there is high temperature and great pressure. The heat and pressure change one kind of rock into another kind of rock. The new rocks become harder than the old rocks. They also look different Sometimes the minerals in the rocks change too.

Some metamorphic rocks also are formed when other rocks come in contact with magma. The magma changes the minerals in the rock.

There are many kinds of metamorphic rocks. Slate is a metamorphic rock. Slate is changed-over shale. Marble is another metamorphic rock. Marble is changed-over limestone.

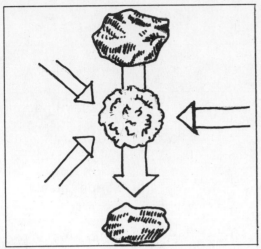

Figure A

Heat and pressure change exising rocks into other rocks. The changed rocks are metamorphic rocks.

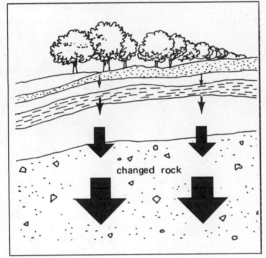

Figure B

Heat and pressure together can change rocks.

The weight of layer upon layer of rocks causes pressure. Pressure builds heat. Heat and pressure change rocks.

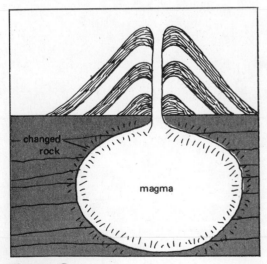

Figure C

Heat, by itself, can change rocks.

Heat from magma may change the rocks next to the magma.

Or, magma may move into cracks or between layers of sedimentary rock. The magma changes the minerals in the rock.

SOME COMMON METAMORPHIC ROCKS

Metamorphic Rocks		Original Rocks	Uses
marble	changed from	limestone	buildings
slate	changed from	shale	roof shingles blackboards slate walks
gneiss	changed from	granite, shale	buildings monuments
schist	changed from	granite, shale, mica	steel-making
quartzite	changed from	sandstone	buildings

Study the chart above and tne answer the questions.

1. What is one use for schist? _____

2. What rocks are changed to form gneiss? _____

3. What rock is changed to form quartzite? _____

4. What is slate used for? _____

5. What metamorphic rock does limestone change to? _____

FILL IN THE BLANK

Complete each statement using a term or terms from the list below. Write your answers in the spaces provided.

slate   marble   igneous
great pressure   harder   steel
look   earth   metamorphic
sedimentary   great heat

1. Rocks formed from melted minerals are called _____ rocks.

2. Rocks formed from sediment are called _____ rocks.

3. Changed-over rocks are called _____ rocks.

4. Two things that can change rocks to other kinds of rocks are _____

   and _____ .

5. Pressure makes rocks become _____ than they were.

6. Heat and pressure can change the way rocks _____ .

7. Metamorphic rocks are formed deep in the _____ .

8. Schist is used to make _____ .

9. Heat and pressure change shale to _____ .

10. Heat and pressure change limestone to _____ .

MATCHING

Match each term in Column A with its descripton in Column B. Write the correct letter in the space provided.

Column A

_____ 1. metamorphic rocks

_____ 2. heat and pressure

_____ 3. slate

_____ 4. marble

_____ 5. deep in the earth

Column B

a) was once shale

b) where metamorphic rocks form

c) changed over rocks

d) was once limestone

e) change rocks

67

TRUE OR FALSE

In the space provided, write "true" if the sentence is true. Write "false" if the sentence is false.

—————— 1. Metamorphic rocks are changed rocks.

—————— 2. Metamorphc rocks are harder than their original rocks.

—————— 3. Only heat can change rocks.

—————— 4. Slate is harder than shale.

—————— 5. Magma can change the minerals in a rock.

—————— 6. Metamorphic rock cannot change to another rock.

—————— 7. Minerals in a rock can change.

—————— 8. Slate changes to shale.

—————— 9. Gneiss is harder than granite.

—————— 10. Only pressure can change rocks.

WHICH CAME FIRST?

In each of the pairs below, one of the things came from the other. On the line next to each pair, write the name of the thing that formed the other.

1. sand or sandstone? _____

2. quartzite or sandstone? _____

3. shale or mud? _____

4. slate or shale? _____

5. granite or gneiss? _____

6. marble or limestone? _____

7. plants or soft coal? _____

8. granite or schist? _____

9. rock salt or halite? _____

10. sedimentary rocks or sediment? _____

What is the rock cycle? 12

rock cycle: series of natural processes by which rocks are slowly changed from one kind of rock to another

LESSON 12 | What is the rock cycle?

January, February, March, April, ... You name the next nine. What about spring, summer, ... ? Which three go next. Months and seasons occur in cycles. A cycle is a series of events that happen over and over.

Nature has many kinds of cycles. The rise and fall of the tides is a cycle that occurs twice each day. Oxygen and carbon dioxide move through the environment in a cycle.

Another natural cycle is the rock cycle. You have learned that there are three classes of rocks, igneous, sedimentary, and metamorphic. However, rocks do not remain in the same form forever. They are constantly changing. In fact, <u>any rock can change to another kind of rock</u>. For example:

- Igneous and sedimentary rocks may be changed to metamorphic rock by great heat and pressure.

- Igneous, metamorphic, and sedimentary rocks can be exposed to the earth's surface. Weathering then breaks them into fragments. The fragments may then form new sedimentary rock.

All kinds of rocks may become buried where temperatures are so high they melt into magma. In time, the magma can cool and harden into igneous rock.

The endless change of the rocks from one form to another is called the **rock cycle**. You can see a diagram of the rock cycle in Figure A on the next page. Notice that rock changes need not take place in any special order. The two-way arrows show that the changes can take place in any order.

Geologists believe that since the earth began about 4 1/2 - 5 million years ago, its crust has undergone several rock cycles.

THE ROCK CYCLE

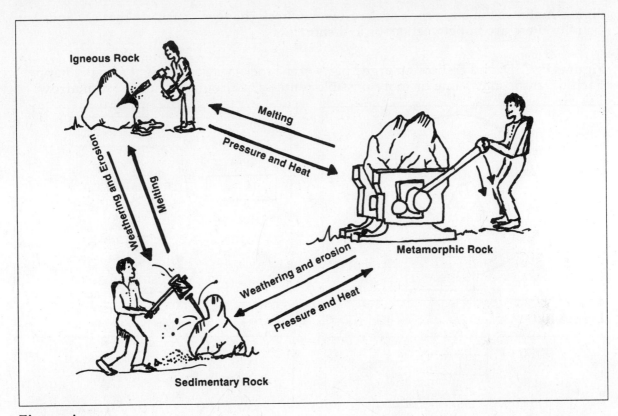

Figure A

Use Figure A to identify the cause or causes for each of the rock changes listed below.

	Change	Cause (or Causes)
1.	Igneous to sedimentary	
2.	Sedimentary to metamorphic	
3.	Sedimentary to igneous	
4.	Metamorphic to igneous	
5.	Igneous to metamorphic	
6.	Metamorphic to sedimentary	

INTERPRETING ROCK CYCLES

Figure A shows the basic rock cycle. However, rock changes are rarely that cut-and-dry. Usually there are in-between steps and shortcuts.

Figures B, C, D, and E show enlarged parts of the rock cycle as it might actually happen. Each diagram shows one or more possible routes. Each route is shown by an arrow.

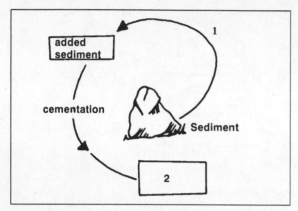

Figure B

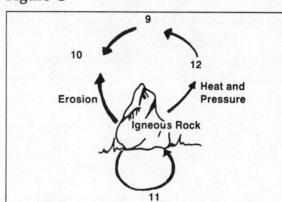

Figure C

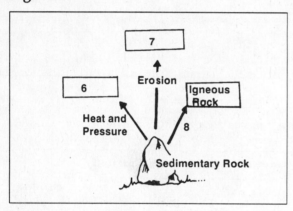

Figure D

Figure E

Fill in the missing term that best describes each number in the diagrams. Choose from the following terms:

heat and pressure	melting and hardening
metamorphic rock	sediment
erosion	sedimentary rock

1. _____   7. _____

2. _____   8. _____

3. _____   9. _____

4. _____   10. _____

5. _____   11. _____

6. _____   12. _____

FILL IN THE BLANK

Complete each statement using a term or terms from the list below. Write your answers in the spaces provided.

rocks   rock cycle   magma
order   metamorphic   igneous
sedimentary   fragments

1. There are three classes of _____.

2. Molten rock material is called _____.

3. Rock formed form rock fragments is called _____ rock.

4. Rock formed from molten minerals is called _____ rock.

5. Rock formed as a result of heat and pressure is called _____ rock.

6. Erosion can break rock into _____.

7. The unending change of rocks from one form to another is called the_____.

8. Rock changes can happen in any _____.

TRUE OR FALSE

In the space provided, write "true" if the sentence is true. Write "false" if the sentence is false.

_____ 1. Weathering changes metamorphic rock to sediments.

_____ 2. Magma cools to form sedimentary rock.

_____ 3. Rocks have been changing since the beginning of the earth.

_____ 4. Rocks are always changing

_____ 5. An increase in temperature will always change an igneous or sedimentary rock to a metamorphic rock.

_____ 6. Igneous rock can only change into sedimentary rock.

_____ 7. Some rocks contain material that were once part of every rock type.

_____ 8. Heat and pressure change sedimentary rock into igneous rock.

SCIENCE *EXTRA*

Growing Cleaner Crystals

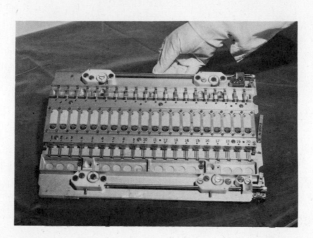

At one time, all watches had to be set and wound up every day. Today, most modern watches are electronic. They operate by electricity supplied by a tiny battery. Do you own a watch? Chances are that it is battery powered. It also is likely that the term "quartz" or "quartz crystal" is printed somewhere on the face of the watch.

Crystals are the key to the electronics industry. Crystals of quartz are semiconductors. A semiconductor is a substance that is neither a conductor nor a non-conductor of electricity. It is "in-between." Such materials can be treated to transmit electricity in precise amounts. Semiconductors are used to manufacture many electronic devices, including transistors, microchips, and integrated circuits. In turn, these devices are used to make radios, television sets, computers and many of the appliances we use today.

Crystals are found in nature. However, natural crystals are not pure enough for electronic use. They contain too many impurities. Scientists have learned how to "grow" clean crystals in the lab. Clean crystals are more reliable and can be used to make smaller and faster electronics. This is especially important for high-tech computers, such as the ones used in scientific research, big business, and space exploration.

However, even "clean" crystals contain some impurities. The race is now on to remove even more of these impurities. Research has shown that crystals grow larger and cleaner in outer space. In outer space, there is little gravity, winds and other "upsetting" influences that are found on the earth.

Research on crystal growth is done on the U.S. Space Shuttle and aboard the Soviet space station *Mir*. Perhaps someday, large crystal growing factories will orbit the Earth. The crystals made in these factories will be so pure that devices that are impossible to build today will be commonplace.

What causes mechanical weathering?

13

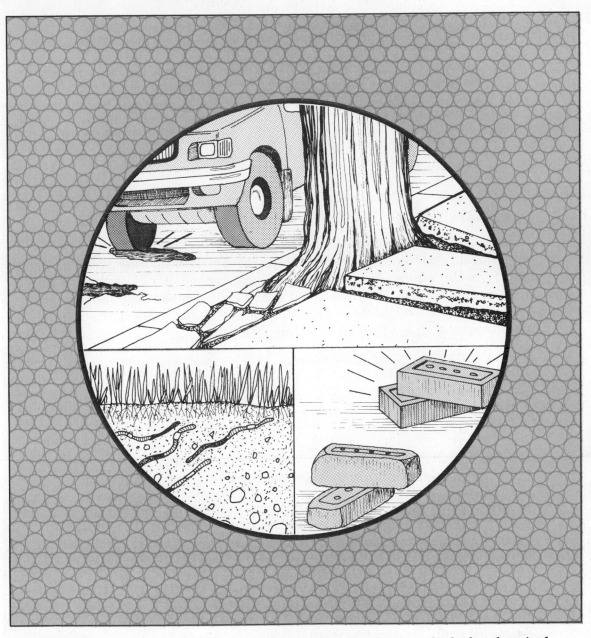

mechanical [muh-KAN-ih-kul] **weathering:** weathering in which the chemical makeup of rocks does not change
weathering: breaking down of rocks and other materials on the earth's surface

LESSON 13 | What causes mechanical weathering?

Ants are very tiny. What can such tiny creatures do to the earth's crust? Plenty! Ants and other animals are helping to break down the earth's crust. They are a cause of **mechanical** [muh-KAN-ih-kul] **weathering.**

Weathering is the name for the breaking down of the earth's crust. Mechanical weathering breaks rocks into smaller and smaller pieces. It does not change the chemicals of the rocks.

There are four main causes of mechanical weathering. They are: temperature changes, frost action, root action, and animal activity.

TEMPERATURE CHANGES: Heat makes most things expand—get bigger. Cold makes most things contract—get smaller. In most places, it is warmer during the day than at night. Heat expands rocks during the day. At night, the rocks cool off and contract. The expanding and contracting happen over and over again. That strains the rocks. The strain makes them crack—a tiny bit at a time.

FROST ACTION: Most things contract when they freeze. Not water! Water expands when it freezes into ice. Rain water seeps into tiny cracks in rocks. When the water freezes, it expands. The ice presses against the sides of the cracks. The pressure is great. It can make cracks bigger. It can even break apart the rocks.

ROOT ACTION: Trees and shrubs have roots that can grow into cracks of rocks. Growing roots are very strong. They can split rocks.

ANIMAL ACTIVITY: Animals do not break rocks apart by themselves. But some animals dig into the ground. Ants, worms, woodchucks, and some others dig holes. The holes let in air and water. The air and water weather the rocks.

COMPLETING SENTENCES

Choose the correct word or term for each statement. Write your choice in the spaces provided.

Figure A

Figure B

1. During the day, rocks _____ .
   expand, contract

2. During the night, rocks _____ .
   expand, contract

3. Repeated contraction and expansion strain rocks. Strain can _____ rocks.
   cool, crack

4. Changes of temperature can cause _____ weathering.
   chemical, mechanical

5. Water _____ seep into cracks easily.
   does, does not

6. Water _____ when it freezes.
   expands, contracts

7. Ice presses against the cracks in rocks. The pressure can _____ rocks.
   contract, crack

8. Frost action is an example of _____ weathering.
   chemical, mechanical

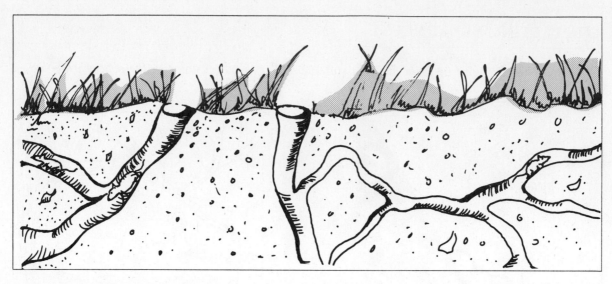

Figure C *A busy world below the ground.*

9.   Animals _____ break rocks apart by themselves.
     do, do not

10. Holes made by animals in the soil let in _____ .
     pressure, air and water

11. Air and water _____ .
     wear down rocks, keep rocks in one piece

Figure D

12. The rock in Figure D was split by _____ .
     roots, ice

13. Root-action is an example of _____ weathering.
     mechanicsl, chemical

14. Mechanical weathering _____ change a rock's chemicals.
     does, does not

15. Mechanical weathering _____ change the size and shape of rocks.
     does, does not

FILL IN THE BLANK

Complete each statement using a term or terms from the list below. Write your answers in the spaces provided.

roots	carry away	mechanical
more	frost action	crack
weathering	pressure	animal activity
root	temperature changes	air
water	holes	

1. The breaking down of the earth's crust is called _____ .

2. Weathering that does not cause chemical changes is called _____ weathering.

3. Four causes of mechanical weathering are _____ ,

    _____ , _____ and _____ action.

4. Heating and cooling over and over again can _____ rocks.

5. When water freezes it takes up _____ room.

6. The _____ of ice can split a rock.

7. Ants, worms, and woodchucks help weathering because they make_____ in the soil.

8. _____ and _____ pass through the holes that animals make in the soil.

9. A plant's _____ can split rocks.

10. Weathering just splits the earth's crust into smaller and smaller pieces. It does not

    _____ the pieces.

MATCHING

Match each term in Column A with its description Column B. Write the correct letter in the space provided.

Column A	Column B
_____ 1. weathering	a) expands rock
_____ 2. water	b) contracts rocks
_____ 3. rise in temperature	c) the breaking down of the earth's crust
_____ 4. drop in temperature	d) the part of a plant that is usually in the ground
_____ 5. roots	e) expands when frozen

79

TRUE OR FALSE

In the space provided, write "true" if the sentence is true. Write "false" if the sentence is false.

_____ 1. Mechanical weathering changes a rock's chemicals.

_____ 2. "Expand" means to become larger.

_____ 3. Heat makes rocks expand.

_____ 4. Rocks expand at night.

_____ 5. Expansion and contraction can strain rocks.

_____ 6. Growing grass roots have no force.

_____ 7. Rocks usually have tiny cracks and holes.

_____ 8. Water can go into tiny openings.

_____ 9. Air and water help weathering.

_____ 10. Woodchucks eat rocks.

REACHING OUT

Figure E

Earthworms burrow through the soil. as they move, they turn over soil. This make the soil better for farming. Why do you think that the earthworm is "one of people's best friends?"

_____

_____

_____

What causes chemical weathering ?

chemical [KEM-ih-kul] **weathering**:   weathering in which the chemical makeup of rocks changes

LESSON 14 | What causes chemical weathering?

Chemical [KEM-ih-kul] **weathering** breaks up rocks. It also changes the chemicals of the rocks. Chemical changes take place when the minerals in rocks are broken down into other substances. A chemically weathered rock may be brittle. It may break easily. You could even break it with your hands.

Chemical weathering has worn down huge parts of the earth's crust. It happens fastest in hot, wet climates. But even "fast" chemical weathering is very slow. To dissolve just 30 meters (100 feet) of limestone takes about 6 million years.

Most chemical weathering is caused by the actions of <u>oxygen,</u> <u>rain water</u>, and <u>acids formed when carbon dioxide and water combine</u>.

OXYGEN in the air links up with some of the elements in rocks. The link-up forms oxides. The oxides break away from the rocks.

One oxide that you probably know well is rust. Rust is iron oxide. Iron is found in many rocks. When oxygen links up with iron, rust (iron oxide) is formed. Rust crumbles easily. Rusted rocks fall apart.

RAIN WATER can change minerals in two ways. **a)** It dissolves some minerals. **b)** Water links up with other minerals. Then new substances are formed. The new substances break away from rocks. And the rocks crumble.

CARBON DIOXIDE in the air dissolves easily in rain water. Water and carbon dioxide form carbonic [kar-BON-ik] acid. Acids dissolve some rocks such as limestone. Carbonic acid has dissolved underground limestone in many places. Mammoth Caves, in Kentucky, was formed by the action of carbonic acid. So was Carlsbad Caverns, in New Mexico.

COMPLETING SENTENCES

Choose the correct word or term for each statement. Write you choice in the spaces provided.

Figure A

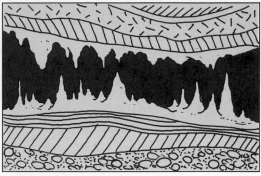

Figure B

1. This rock in Figure A is "rusting"

    a) Rust forms when _____ links up with _____ .

limestone, iron   oxygen, carbon dioxide

    b) The iron comes from the rock. Where does the oxygen come from?

    _____

the air, rain

2. The chemical name for rust is _____ .

carbon oxide, iron oxide

3. What kind of weather speeds rusting? _____

cold and dry, warm and moist

4. Rusting is an example of _____ weathering.

mechanical, chemical

5. What dissolved the limestone to form the caves shown in Figure B?

    _____

carbon dioxide, carbonic acid

6. Carbonic acid forms when _____ combines with _____ .

carbon dioxide, oxygen   iron, water

7. Carbon dioxide comes from _____ .

water, the air

8. The dissolving of limestone is an example of _____ weathering.

mechanical, chemical

9. Chemical weathering _____ change the chemicals in rocks.

does, does not

10. Chemical weathering _____ form new products.

does, does not

MECHANICAL OR CHEMICAL WEATHERING

Study each diagram below which shows causes of weathering. Then answer the questions about each diagram.

Figure C

Figure D

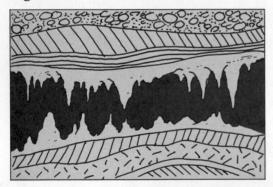

Figure E

Figure F

1. Figure C shows and example of

   _____ weathering.
   <u>mechanical, chemical</u>

2. The chemical make-up of the crust

   _____ changing.
   <u>is, is not</u>

3. Figure D shows an example of

   _____ weathering.
   <u>mechanical, chemical</u>

4. The chemical make-up of the the

   crust _____ changing.
   <u>is, is not</u>

5. Figure E shows an example of

   _____ weathering.
   <u>mechanical, chemical</u>

6. The chemical make-up of the crust

   _____ changing.
   <u>is, is not</u>

7. Figure F shows an example of

   _____ weathering.
   <u>mechanical, chemical</u>

8. The chemical make-up of the crust

   _____ changing.
   <u>is, is not</u>

FILL IN THE BLANK

Complete each statement using a term or terms from the list below. Write your answers in the spaces provided. Some words may be used more than once.

the air   oxide   new products
oxygen   speeds   crumbles
underground caves rain water   rust
carbon dioxide   carbonic acid

1. Most chemical weathering is caused by the actions of _____ ,

   _____ and _____ .

2. Chemical weathering always forms _____ .

3. Oxygen links up with iron to form the compound called iron _____ .

4. Another name for iron oxide is _____ .

5. Rust _____ easily.

6. The oxygen that rusts iron come from _____ .

7. Carbonic acid is formed when _____ dissolves in water.

8. Carbon dioxide comes from _____ .

9. Dissolved limestone may form _____ .

10. Hot, moist weather _____ chemical weathering.

MATCHING

Match each term in Column A with its description in Column B. Write the correct letter in the space provided.

Column A	Column B
_____ 1. rust	a) form carbonic acid
_____ 2. water and carbon dioxide	b) dissolves limestone
_____ 3. cold, dry climate	c) speeds chemical weathering
_____ 4. carbonic acid	d) iron oxide
_____ 5. warm, moist climate	e) slows chemical weathering

TRUE OR FALSE

In the space provided, write "true" if the sentence is true. Write "false" if the sentence is false.

_____ 1. Mechanical weathering changes the chemicals of rocks.

_____ 2. Chemical weathering changes the chemicals of rocks.

_____ 3. Chemical weathering happens very fast.

_____ 4. All rocks contain iron.

_____ 5. Rust crumbles easily.

_____ 6. Water alone can weather some rocks.

_____ 7. Carbonic acid dissolves every mineral.

_____ 8. Carbonic acid forms from carbon dioxide and iron.

_____ 9. Carbonic acid dissolves limestone.

_____ 10. The scientific name for rust is iron oxide

WORD SCRAMBLE

Below are several scrambled words you have used in this Lesson. Unscramble the words and write your answers in the spaces provided.

1. ETWAR _____

2. TURS _____

3. NORI _____

4. NAIR _____

5. TONESMILE _____

REACHING OUT

Look back at Figure B on page 83. What may happen if too much limestone dissolves?

_____

_____

How does running water cause erosion?

15

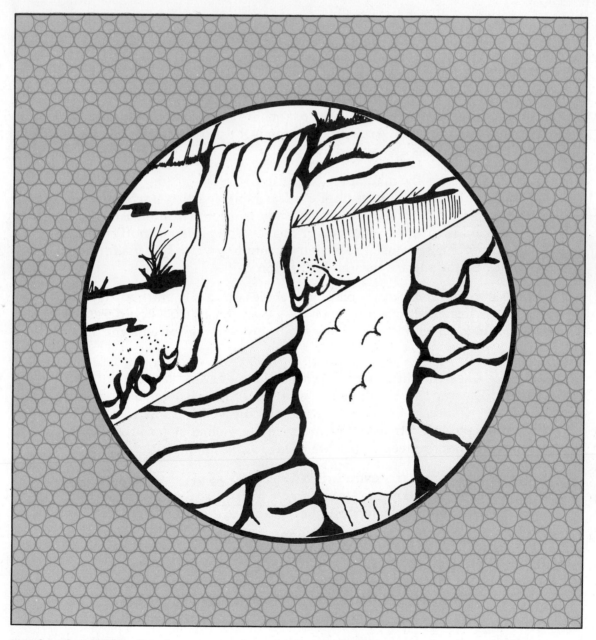

erosion [ee-ROH-zhun]:   process by which weathered material is moved from one
place to another
runoff: rainwater that flows into streams and rivers

LESSON 15 | How does running water cause erosion?

Weathering breaks down rocks, but weathering does not carry away the pieces of rock. What carries the pieces away?

Another process moves the pieces of rock from one place to another. It is called **erosion** [ee-ROH-zhun]. Erosion is the process by which pieces of weathered rocks are carried away.

Running water is the main force of erosion. Rivers, streams and **runoff**, change the surface of the earth. Runoff is rainwater that flows over the earth's surface. During heavy rains there is a lot of runoff. As runoff flows over the earth's surface, it carries away soil pieces. Runoff empties into rivers and streams. The action of running water has made more changes on the surface than any other force.

Water in rivers and streams picks up pebbles, sand, silt, and clay. It even picks up heavier fragments, such as gravel, rocks, and boulders. All these things act as abrasives. They scrape away at the bottoms and sides of streams.

Speed makes the difference. The faster a stream moves, the more it carries. The more material the stream carries, the faster the bottom and sides of the stream are eroded. Streams flow very fast when they go down steep slopes. Streams flow more slowly when they go down gentle slopes. Therefore, steep slopes are eroded faster than gentle slopes.

Sometimes steams carry extra water. That happens in time of heavy rain. The extra water makes the stream move faster. Because it is faster, the water picks up more material and causes more erosion.

Streams are the greatest force of erosion. They have worn away large parts of our earth's surface.

The Grand Canyon was once flat land. The land was eroded away by the Colorado River.

In some places the canyon is 1830 meters (6000) deep.

It took the Colorado River about 30 million years to erode so much land.

Even today, the river is slowly making the canyon deeper and wider.

Find the Colorado River in the photo. It is not very large. . . but it is <u>very powerful</u>.

Figure A

Figure B

Water enters a stream in three ways. Some rain falls directly into the stream. Some runoff water flows off from the top of the ground. Other water seeps in from under the ground.

A river system is made up of one main stream and all the streams that flow into it.

Study the diagrams below. Then answer the questions under each diagram.

Figure C

Figure D

Figures C and D show two different streams. Which stream . . .

1. is moving down a gentle slope? _____

2. is moving down a steep slope? _____

3. is moving faster? _____

4. is moving slower? _____

5. carries more sediment? _____

6. carries less sediment? _____

7. erodes more? _____

8. erodes less? _____

Conclusions:

1. Water flowing down a steep slope moves _____ than water flowing down a gentle slope.
    <small>slower, faster</small>

2. Fast moving water carries _____ sediment than slow moving
water.
    <small>more, less</small>

3. Fast moving water erodes _____ than slow moving water.
    <small>more, less</small>

Figure E

Figure F

Figures E and F show the same stream at different times. In which diagram is the stream . . .

1. carrying more water? _____

2. carrying less water ? _____

3. moving faster? _____

4. moving slower? _____

5. carrying more sediment? _____

6. carrying less sediment? _____

7. eroding more? _____

8. eroding less? _____

Conclusions:

1. During heavy rain, a stream carries _____ water.

more, less

2. During heavy rain, a stream moves _____ .

faster, slower

3. During heavy rain, a stream carries _____ sediment.

more, less

4. During heavy rain, erosion by a stream _____ .

increases, decreases

5. During heavy rain, the water level of a stream _____ .

rises, falls

FILL IN THE BLANK

Complete each statement using a term or terms from the list below. Write your answers in the spaces provided. Some words may be used more than once.

more   erode   faster
particles   breaks down   less
carried away   running water   downhill

1. Weathering only _____ rocks.

2. Erosion is the process by which pieces of rock are _____ .

3. The main force of erosion is _____ .

4. In times of heavy rain, sometimes streams carry _____ water.

5. Streams carry all kinds of _____ .

6. Materials carried by streams _____ the sides and bottom of the stream.

7. Streams move only in a _____ direction.

8. Steep streams move _____ than gently sloping streams.

9. Steep streams carry _____ particles than gently sloping streams.

10. Gently sloping streams erode _____ than steep streams.

MATCHING

Match each term in Column A with its description in Column B. Write the correct letter in the space provided.

Column A

_____ 1. running water

_____ 2. runoff

_____ 3. erosion

_____ 4. steep slope

_____ 5. gentle slope

Column B

a) fast-moving stream

b) main force of erosion

c) slow-moving stream

d) carrying away of weathered rock pieces

e) empties into rivers and streams

TRUE OR FALSE

In the space provided, write "true" if the sentence is true. Write "false" if the sentence is false.

_____ **1.** During heavy rain, there is less runoff.

_____ **2.** Running water is the most important force of erosion.

_____ **3.** All streams carry sediment.

_____ **4.** All streams flow at the same speed.

_____ **5.** A slow moving stream erodes faster than a fast moving stream.

_____ **6.** A steep stream flows faster than a gently sloping stream.

_____ **7.** A steep stream erodes less than a gently sloping stream.

_____ **8.** Fast moving streams carry more sediment than slow moving streams.

_____ **9.** Heavy rain makes streams erode faster.

_____ **10.** Streams get their water from rain.

WORD SCRAMBLE

Below are several scrambled words you have used in this Lesson. Unscramble the words and write your answers in the spaces provided.

1. SINEROO _____

2. TENDIMES _____

3. SMEART _____

4. DANS _____

5. VRELGA _____

6. OPLES _____

7. ONFURF _____

8. ERSRVI _____

9. DEPSE _____

10. RWTAE _____

WORD SEARCH

The list on the left contains words that you have used in this Lesson. Find and circle each word where it appears in the box. The spellings may go in any direction: up, down, left, right, or diagonally.

WEATHERING

CHEMICAL

MECHANICAL

FROST

ROOTS

ANIMAL

OXIDE

EROSION

STREAM

WATER

O	X	E	I	L	S	E	L	O	W	I	D	W
S	E	R	O	S	I	O	N	E	H	W	O	I
E	W	G	A	N	I	M	A	L	C	E	N	N
G	Y	C	L	S	O	T	D	S	E	A	A	T
F	L	D	H	A	H	R	E	N	D	T	M	A
R	L	O	M	E	C	H	A	N	I	C	A	L
O	I	N	R	X	M	I	N	E	X	W	E	K
S	M	I	E	O	R	I	E	E	O	A	R	N
T	N	E	T	I	O	X	C	R	L	N	T	A
G	A	N	A	X	N	T	E	A	W	E	S	R
R	E	I	W	A	L	G	S	E	L	R	H	F

REACHING OUT

Would planting trees on a hillside help to prevent running water from eroding the land? Explain.

_____

_____

_____

_____

What are flood plains and deltas?

delta: triangular-shaped deposit of sediment located at the mouth of a river
flood plain: flat area on the side of a river where sediments are deposited during floods

LESSON 16 | What are flood plains and deltas?

Running water carries sediment. But it does not carry sediment forever. Sooner or later, the sediment must settle. Some streams may carry sediment very far. At some time, however, the streams will deposit the sediment.

The sediment that streams deposit, builds up land areas. Two kinds of land areas that are built up by sediment are **flood plains** and **deltas.**

FLOOD PLAINS

After a heavy rain, a stream carries more water than usual. This raises the water level. Sometimes the level gets so high that the water flows over its channel—the place it usually flows through. Then there is flooding.

The flood water deposits fine sediment on the banks, which is land next to the stream. Some streams flood often. The sediment builds up flat areas called flood plains. Soil on flood plains is very good for farming.

DELTAS

Almost every stream empties its water into a larger body of water. It empties into a larger river or an ocean. The place where a stream empties its water is called the mouth.

A stream flows slowly at the mouth. It deposits its sediment at the mouth. The sediment builds large land areas, called deltas. A delta is shaped like a triangle. It gets its name from the Greek letter "delta" (Δ). What does the Greek delta look like?

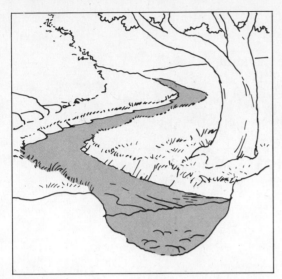

Figure A

Usually, stream water stays in the channel. It does not flow onto its banks.

Figure B

In times of heavy rain, however, the water may flow over its channel.

Flood water deposits fine sediment on both banks of a stream. The sediment builds flood plains.

Figure C

1. Flood plain soil is very fertile. There are many good farms on flood plains. *BUT* the

   farmers are taking a big chance. Why? _____

   _____

   _____

2. Would you want to live on a flood plain? _____

3. Explain why or why not. _____

   _____

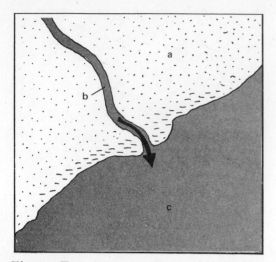

Figure D

Imagine yourself looking down from high in the sky.

"a" is land
"b" is a stream
"c" is a large body of water

The stream empties into the water.

The stream deposits its sediment at its mouth. The sediment builds up. All the sediment is under water.

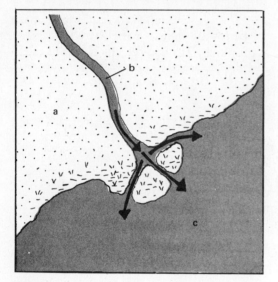

Figure E

The sediment builds up and up. Much of it reaches above the water level. Much is now even with the land. The sediment is now "new" land.

The stream has cut new channels across this new land.

How many new channels do you see? _____

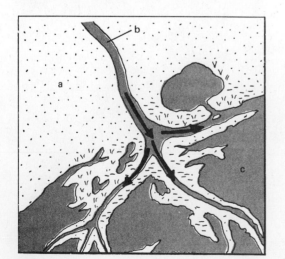

Figure F

The build-up continues. More sediment is deposited. More land builds up. The land grows outward in the shape of a delta (Δ). It will continue to grow.

Why will the delta keep growing? _____

_____

_____

FILL IN THE BLANK

Complete each statement using a term or terms from the list below. Write your answers in the spaces provided. Some words may be used more than once.

deposited   deltas   erosion
slowly   flooding   mouth
flood plains   delta   farming
channel

1. The process by which parts of the earth's crust are carried away is called

   _____.

2. Material that is eroded eventually is _____.

3. Soil on flood plains is good for _____.

4. The part of a stream that the water flows through is called the _____.

5. Stream sediment builds land areas called _____ and _____.

6. When water overflows its channel, _____ takes place.

7. Fine sediment laid down during floods builds a _____.

8. The place where a stream empties its water is called its _____.

9. The water at the mouth of a stream usually flows _____.

10. Sediment deposited at the mouth of a stream builds a _____.

MATCHING

Match each term in Column A with its description in Column B. Write the correct letter in the space provided.

Column A		Column B	
_____ 1.	flood plain	a)	shape of a delta
_____ 2.	delta	b)	built by flood sediment
_____ 3.	channel	c)	built at mouth of stream
_____ 4.	triangle	d)	stream's end
_____ 5.	mouth	e)	place a stream usually flows through

TRUE OR FALSE

In the space provided, write "true" if the sentence is true. Write "false" if the sentence is false.

_____ 1. Most streams empty into a larger body of water.

_____ 2. All streams carry sediment.

_____ 3. The slower a stream moves, the more sediment it carries.

_____ 4. A stream deposits its sediment when it speeds up.

_____ 5. Flood plains build up at the mouths of streams.

_____ 6. A river bank is at the end of a river.

_____ 7. Heavy sediment settles before fine sediment.

_____ 8. A delta keeps growing.

_____ 9. Heavy rain always causes flooding.

_____ 10. A stream flows slowly at its mouth.

WORD SCRAMBLE

Below are several scrambled words you have used in this Lesson. Unscramble the words and write your answers in the spaces provided.

1. SDMNTEIE _____

2. FLDOPLNOAI _____

3. DLTAE _____

4. TRNGLAIE _____

5. MTHUO _____

How do glaciers change the earth's surface?

glacier [GLAY-shur]:   moving river of ice and snow
moraine [moor-AYN]:   ridge of till deposited by a retreating glacier
till: rock material deposited by a glacier

LESSON 17 | How do glaciers change the earth's surface?

In some places, it is always cold. On very high mountains, and in the polar regions, it never rains. It only snows, and the snow never melts. It piles up and up. It becomes higher and higher. In time, the snow changes to ice. And the ice layer becomes thicker and thicker. When it gets very, very thick, the weight of the ice makes it move. Slowly it creeps forward—like a frozen moving mountain. We call a giant sheet of ice and snow moving on land, a **glacier** [GLAY-shur].

Glaciers erode the earth. They have changed the shape of large parts of the earth's surface. They are still making changes, even today. Little by little, glaciers break off large parts of the crust and carry them away. They make valleys wider and deeper. They wear down mountains and change their shapes.

How do glaciers do this? As glaciers move down rocky valleys, they pick up assorted fragments. Some are as large as boulders. Most are smaller. They include rocks, pebbles, sand, and even dust. Material carried by glaciers acts as abrasives. They erode other rocks on the floor and sides of the valley.

Glaciers erode, but they also build. When a glacier reaches a warm place, it melts. Rocks that were frozen into the ice are left behind. The material deposited by a glacier is called **till**. The till builds up a long, low ridge. This ridge is called a **moraine** [moor-AYN]. When a glacier melts, it's till may also pile up as <u>mounds</u>, and large <u>flat areas</u>.

Many huge glaciers have grown and spread and then melted in the past million years. Glaciers grow and spread during <u>ice ages</u>. An ice age is a period of very cold temperature. You may be surprised to learn that large parts of the United States were once covered by huge glaciers.

The last ice age ended about 11,000 years ago. Scientists believe that some day the glaciers will advance again. But do not panic! Do not rush for an ice shovel! The next ice age will not happen for a very long time.

Figure A *This glacier is moving along a valley. It is making the valley wider and deeper.*

Figure B *A valley before glacial erosion.*

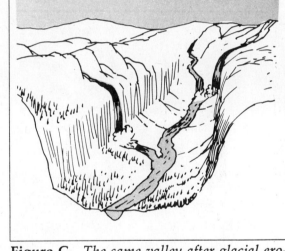

Figure C *The same valley after glacial erosion.*

1. Are there streams?_____

2. Are there waterfalls? _____

3. The shape of the valley is like the

   letter _____
   _{u, v}

4. Are there streams?_____

5. Are there waterfalls? _____

6. NOW the shape of the valley is like

   the letter_____
   _{u, v}

7. Glacial erosion changes _____ shaped valleys to _____
   _{u, v}   _{u, v}
   shaped valleys.

8. Glacial erosion _____ waterfalls.
   _{creates, destroys}

103

Figure D

This mountain was not always this shape. Large parts of the mountain were ripped off by the force of the glacier.

Figure E

North America during the last Ice Age . . . The white area shows the places that were covered by glaciers. The arrows show the direction the glaciers moved.

Figure F

Parts of the basins of the Great Lakes were dug out by a glacier.

Water from the melted glacier filled the basins.

FILL IN THE BLANK

Complete each statement using a term or terms from the list below. Write your answers in the spaces provided. Some words may be used more than once.

ice	the United States	rub
till	slowly	carry off
pressure of its own weight	rocks	widen
break away	snow	thousands
	deepen	pebbles

1. Glaciers are made up of _____ and _____.

2. A glacier may be _____ of meters thick.

3. A glacier moves because of the _____.

4. Glaciers move very _____.

5. Glaciers _____ and _____ big chunks of the earth's crust.

6. Examples of material carried by glaciers are _____ and

   _____.

7. Fragments carried by glaciers _____ against rocks underneath them.

8. Material deposited by a glacier is called _____.

9. Glaciers _____ and _____ valleys.

10. Large parts of _____ were once covered by glaciers.

MATCHING

Match each term in Column A with its description in Column B. Write the correct letter in the space provided.

Column A	Column B
_____ 1. glacier	a) makes a glacier move
_____ 2. pressure of its own weight	b) made wider and deeper by glaciers
_____ 3. moraine	c) ended about 11,000 years ago
_____ 4. valleys	d) giant sheet of moving ice
_____ 5. last ice age	e) long, narrow ridge

TRUE OR FALSE

In the space provided, write "true" if the sentence is true. Write "false" if the sentence is false.

_____ **1.** Snow pressed together can change to ice.

_____ **2.** A glacier moves by itself.

_____ **3.** Glaciers are small.

_____ **4.** A glacier is very powerful.

_____ **5.** Glaciers carry only small rock fragments.

_____ **6.** Glaciers only erode.

_____ **7.** Glaciers build mountains.

_____ **8.** Glaciers change "U"-shaped valleys to "V"-shaped valleys.

_____ **9.** The Great Lakes were formed by glaciers.

_____ **10.** There has been only one ice age.

REACHING OUT

The polar regions are covered with ice and snow. What would happen if all this snow and

ice melted? _____

_____

Figure G

An iceberg is a huge broken-off piece of a glacier floating in the ocean.

Everyone knows that the ocean is salty. And no one should drink salt water.

Now imagine this . . . You are on an iceberg, and you need water to drink.

1. Would you melt part of the iceberg to get this water? _____
yes, no

2. Explain your answer. _____

_____

How does wind change the earth's surface?

dunes: deposits of sand
loess [LESS]: deposits of wind-blown dust

LESSON 18 | How does wind change the earth's surface?

Did the wind ever blow your hat away? Did you ever drop your notebook on a windy day? How many important pages did you lose? Wind is moving air. It can pick up loose materials and carry them far away.

Wind is a force of erosion. It can remove loose materials such as sand and dust particles from the earth's surface. However, wind itself does not erode much. Most "wind" erosion is done by particles carried by wind.

Wind picks up sand particles. When they are blown against rocks they act like abrasives. The sand particles grind the rocks like sandpaper. This happens over and over again. Little by little, the rocks wear down.

The particles carried by wind erode. They also build. What is worn away in one place settles somewhere else.

When wind slows down, it drops the material it is carrying. When sand is dropped, it builds up mounds called **dunes.** Sand dunes are common in deserts and on beaches. Some dunes can cause great damage. They can bury farms and homes, even whole towns.

Wind carries dust higher and farther than it carries sand. Thick deposits of wind-blown dust may build up. The wind-blown dust is called **loess** [LESS]. Some places loess deposits are found are Washington state and Oregon.

Sometimes people plant grasses and shrubs to try to stop wind erosion. How does this help? The roots of plants help to hold down soil and other particles found on the ground.

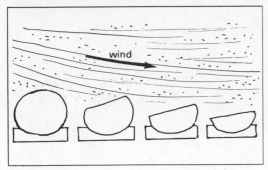

Figure A

Wind erosion wears pebbles and rocks into sharp, flat forms.

Figure A shows the stages of erosion. The sand carried by the wind wears down the rocks little by little.

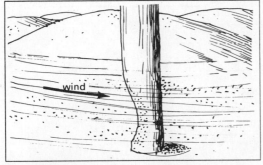

Figure B

Most wind erosion takes place only a few feet off the ground.

In time, what will happen to this pole?_____

_____

Figure C

Sand dunes come in many sizes.

Some dunes are only a meter (3 1/3 ft) high. Others are hundreds of meters high and many kilometers long

Figure D

The Sahara Desert has gigantic dunes.

FILL IN THE BLANK

Complete each statement using a term or terms from the list below. Write your answers in the spaces provided.

beaches   sand   roots
build up   deposited   erosion
loess   deserts   planting grasses and shrubs
dust   abrasives   dunes

1. Wind is a force of _____.

2. Thick deposits of wind-blown dust is called _____.

3. Winds pick up and carry light-weight materials like _____ and

  _____.

4. Sand dunes are common in _____ and on _____.

5. Winds not only wear away, they also _____.

6. Material eroded in one place is _____ somewhere else.

7. Winds deposit sand in mounds called _____.

8. When sand particles are blown against rocks, they act as _____.

9. Wind erosion is sometimes controlled by _____.

10. The _____ of grasses and shrubs help hold soil together.

MATCHING

Match each term in Column A with its description in Column B. Write the correct letter in the space provided.

Column A

_____ 1. wind

_____ 2. dunes

_____ 3. sand and dust

_____ 4. plants

_____ 5. loess

Column B

a) carried by wind

b) wind-blown dust deposits

c) help control wind erosion

d) a force of erosion

e) built by sand particles laid down by wind

TRUE OR FALSE

In the space provided, write "true" if the sentence is true. Write "false" if the sentence is false.

_____ 1. Wind only erodes.

_____ 2. Wind is a force of erosion only in dry places. (Careful, this one is tricky).

_____ 3. Deserts are found in dry places.

_____ 4. All eroded material must be deposited.

_____ 5. Dunes are made of large rocks.

_____ 6. Wind can move dunes from place to place.

_____ 7. Dunes are found only in deserts.

_____ 8. Roots help keep soil together.

_____ 9. Loess is made up of dust.

_____ 10. Wind itself causes much erosion.

WORD SEARCH

The list on the left contains words that you have used in this Lesson. Find and circle each word where it appears in the box. The spellings may go in any direction: up, down, right, or diagonally.

RAIN

SAND

FLOOD

DELTA

CHANNEL

MORAINE

GLACIER

WIND

DUNE

S	P	D	G	A	R	Y	L	E	S	G	R	J
I	A	O	P	A	T	F	L	O	P	E	D	E
L	E	N	L	B	A	T	R	E	T	A	W	R
L	L	T	D	O	M	O	R	A	I	N	E	R
Y	I	E	N	A	W	S	W	A	M	P	R	Y
F	E	A	T	L	E	D	A	T	A	E	D	N
O	L	M	D	U	N	E	D	N	I	W	O	E
R	N	O	T	U	D	I	O	C	H	A	N	L
A	G	I	O	N	S	W	A	M	I	Q	A	E
N	O	R	E	D	P	L	G	R	S	E	Y	H
E	G	D	A	L	G	L	E	N	N	A	H	C

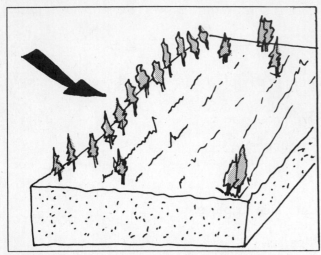

Figure E

Plant roots help hold soil together. How can shrub and tree branches also helphold soil together? _____

_____

_____

Figure F

Scratches from glaciers have been found on many desert rocks. What does this tell us about the earth's climate? _____

_____

_____

How do waves change the earth's surface?

sea arch: gap formed when waves cut completely through a section of rock
sea cave: hollowed out part of a sea cliff
sea cliff: steep rock face caused by wave erosion
sea stack: column of rock remaining after the collapse of a sea arch

LESSON 19 | How do waves change the earth's surface?

Have you ever gone swimming in an ocean? If you have been in the ocean, you probably remember the waves. A wave can knock you down.

The waves in the ocean are very powerful. Even small waves can be very strong, stronger than they look.

Most waves are formed when wind blows over the water. The stronger the wind, the larger the waves.

Waves change the shoreline. Day and night, waves pound against the shore. Little by little, they break up rocks into small pieces. The pieces are abrasives. They grind away and cut into the shoreline. This wears down the rocks more and particles of sand are formed. The sand is then carried away by waves.

As you have probably guessed, waves not only wear away and erode, they also build. Material carried away from one place is deposited somewhere else.

Waves carry rock particles and other materials away from a shoreline. This material may be deposited at another place. A beach is formed when sand and rock particles are deposited on a shoreline by waves.

Waves move in from the ocean to the shore. However, some ocean water moves along the shore. The water that follows the shoreline is called a long shore current.

Long shore currents can carry sand away from the beach. In addition, shore currents also build up parts of the shoreline.

Waves are always changing the shorelines. They are always causing erosion in some places and building up other places.

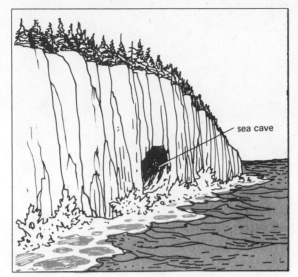

Figure A

Figure B

Waves pound against the bottom of the rocks on a rocky shoreline. A **sea cliff** is formed. A sea cliff is a steep rock face caused by wind erosion. When waves erode the softer rock in a sea cliff, a **sea cave** is formed.

Sometimes a sea cave is worn away all the way through the cliff. This "hole" in a cliff forms a **sea arch**. A sea arch looks like a natural bridge.

Figure C

In time, the top of a sea arch may fall into the water. The remaining columns of rock are called **sea stacks**.

Figure D

Beaches are built of material eroded by waves and deposited on the shore. Materials that form beaches may vary in size and shape. For example, pebble beaches are found along some shorelines. Along the east and west coasts, weathered quartz forms white sand beaches.

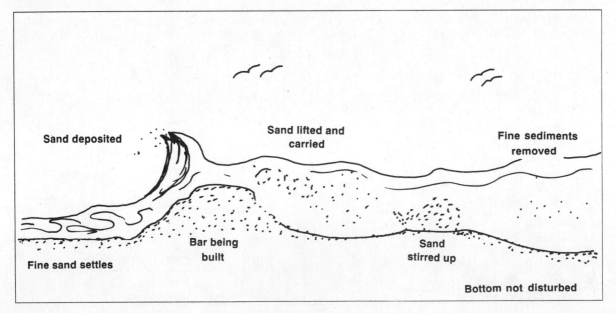

Figure E

Waves carry much sand away from a beach, especially during the winter. This sand is dropped offshore and builds up parallel to the shoreline. It forms low ridges called <u>sand bars</u>.
Sand bars are mostly under water and not far from shore. Sand bars slow down waves. The water between a sand bar and the shore usually is quiet. The quiet water between a sand bar and the shore is called a <u>lagoon</u>.

THE WORK OF SHORE CURRENTS

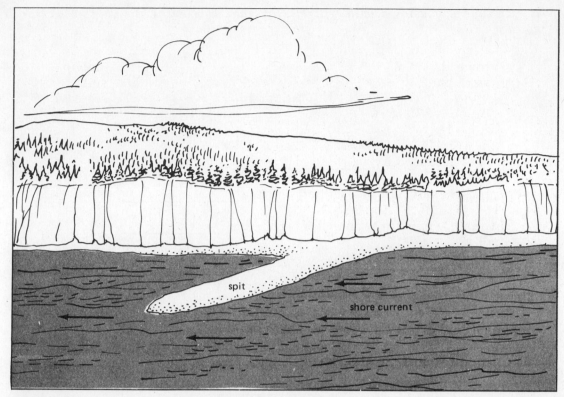

Figure F

Long shore currents erode beaches. Sand and pebbles are carried away. Then they are deposited. The particles may build up finger-like pieces of land called spits.

One end of a spit is connected to the land. The other end reaches out to the ocean.

WORD SCRAMBLE

Below are several scrambled words you have used in this Lesson. Unscramble the words and write your answers in the spaces provided.

1. SWEAV   _____

2. KACST   _____

3. TIPS   _____

4. GOLNOA   _____

5. STRUNREC   _____

FILL IN THE BLANK

Complete each statement using a term or terms from the list below. Write your answers in the spaces provided.

towards   along   lagoon
sand bars   sea stack   spits
wind   sea arch   sea cave
beaches

1. Most waves are caused by _____.

2. Waves can carve out part of a cliff and form a _____.

3. A sea cave that wears through a cliff is called a _____.

4. When the top of a sea arch collapses, a _____ is left.

5. Waves move _____ the shore.

6. Long shore currents move _____ the shore.

7. Sediment laid down by waves on shore build _____.

8. Waves build ridges of sand called _____.

9. Long shore currents build up _____.

10. The quiet water between a sand bar and the shore is called a _____.

MATCHING

Match each term in Column A with its description in Column B. Write the correct letter in the space provided.

Column A

_____ 1. lagoon

_____ 2. waves

_____ 3. long shore currents

_____ 4. beaches

_____ 5. finger-like land form

Column B

a) caused by wind

b) built by waves

c) quite water between the shore and a sand bar

d) spit

e) move along the shore

WHICH CAME FIRST?

In each of the pairs below, one of the things came before the other. One the line next to each pair. write the name of the thing that came before the other.

1. rocks or sand? _____

2. sand or pebbles? _____

3. sea arch or sea cave? _____

4. wind or waves? _____

5. spit or sand? _____

6. beaches or waves? _____

7. sea cliff or sea cave? _____

8. sea cliff or sea stack? _____

9. erosion or fragments? _____

10. sea stack or sea cave? _____

TRUE OR FALSE

In the space provided, write "true" if the sentence is true. Write "false" if the sentence is false.

_____ 1. Waves only erode.

_____ 2. Long shore currents only erode.

_____ 3. Long shore currents move along the shoreline.

_____ 4. Waves move along the shoreline.

_____ 5. Beaches are built from material eroded by waves.

_____ 6. Sea arches are carved by waves.

_____ 7. All beaches have white sand.

_____ 8. A lagoon is a body of land.

_____ 9. Water in a lagoon is very choppy.

_____ 10. Most waves are caused by wind

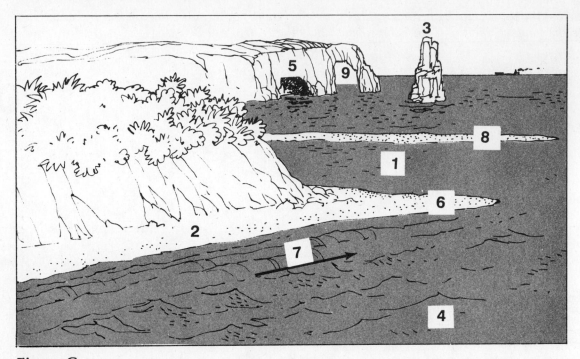

Figure G

Name the features shown above. Search back in the Lesson if necessary.

1. _____

2. _____

3. _____

4. _____

5. _____

6. _____

7. _____

8. _____

9. _____

REACHING OUT

Most waves are caused by wind. What else do you think causes waves?

_____

_____

_____

What is the theory of continental drift?

20

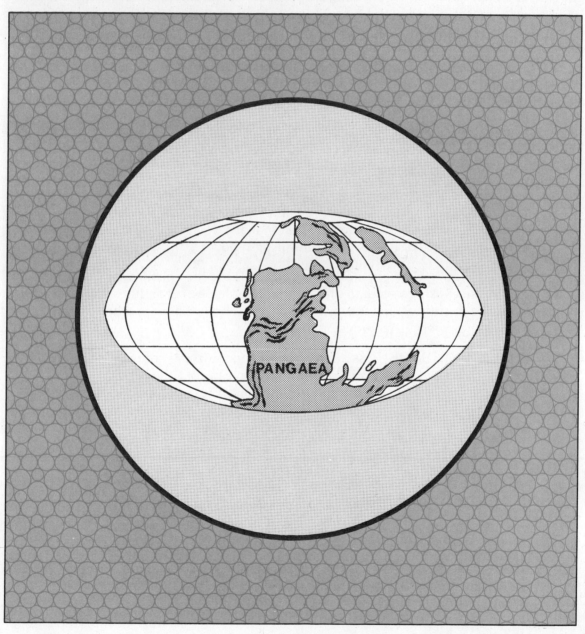

continental [KAHNT-un-ent-ul] **drift:** idea that states the continents were once a giant land mass, and broke into pieces that moved to the positions they are in today

LESSON 20 | What is the theory of continental drift?

You may find it hard to believe, but the seven continents are <u>moving</u>. A continent is a large land mass. In fact, most scientists think that at one time, there was only <u>one</u> giant continent. It was named <u>Pangaea</u> [pan-JEE-uh]. Pangaea is Greek for "all the land." Then, about 200 million years ago, Pangaea began to break apart. The pieces began to move apart. They become today's seven continents. How fast did the pieces move? VERY SLOWLY — no more than 2 1/2 centimeters each year. Today the continents continue to move.

The idea that the continents were once part of a giant land mass is called **continental** [KAHNT-un-ent-ul] **drift**. It was first stated in 1912 by Alfred Wegener, a German scientist.

Wegener based his idea of continental drift upon his study of the coastlines of the continents. He noticed that in many places, coastlines seemed to fit together, like pieces of a giant jigsaw puzzle.

Look at Figure C on the next page. Notice how the coastlines of South America and Africa seem to fit together. The shape of coastlines is strong evidence to support the theory of continental drift. There is other strong evidence as well. It includes:

FOSSIL EVIDENCE Fossils are the remains of living things that lived long ago. Similar plant and animal fossils have been discovered in places that are far apart, in matching coastlines on different continents.

MOUNTAIN EVIDENCE Some mountain ranges on different continents seem to match. For example, a mountain range in eastern Canada seems to match one found in Norway and Sweden. The mountains would have separated when the continents started drifting apart.

ROCK EVIDENCE The age and kind of rocks and minerals along the edge of one continent match rocks and minerals along the edge of another continent.

Most scientists support the theory of continental drift. Some, however, are not convinced. They point to evidence and questions that this theory cannot explain.

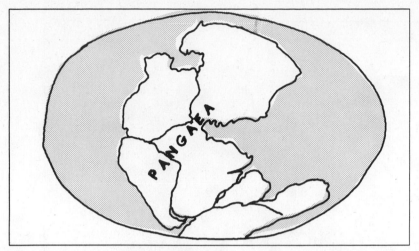

200 million years ago one giant land mass existed

Figure A *200 Million Years Ago*

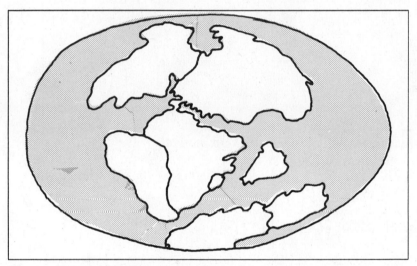

The land mass was breaking apart. The pieces slowly drifted apart.

Figure B *135 Million Years Ago*

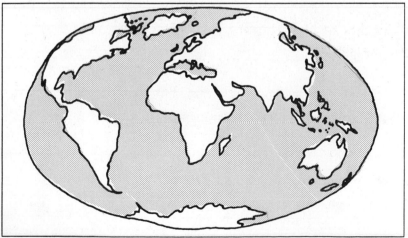

Today the pieces are the seven continents.

Figure C *Today*

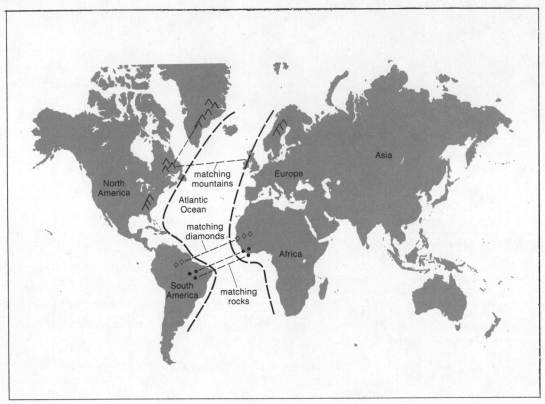

Figure D *Matching Mountains, Rocks, and Diamonds (a mineral)*

Study Figures A, B, C, and D. Then answer the following questions on the lines provided.

1. What was the giant landmass of 200 million years ago called?

   _____

2. How do the shapes of different coastlines support continental drift?

   _____

3. Which continents seem to fit together? _____

   _____

4. Name two continents on which matching rocks and minerals are found.

   _____

5. Name two continents on which matching moutains are found?

   _____

FILL IN THE BLANK

Complete each statement using a term or terms from the list below. Write your answers in the spaces provided. Some words may be used more than once.

mountain ranges   Wegener   continental drift
one   Pangaea   200 million
years   coastlines   rocks and minerals
fossils   continues   move apart

1. More than 200 million years ago, the earth had only _____ large land mass.

2. The earth's original landmass is called _____ .

3. About 200 million years ago, the earth's single land mass broke up and started slowly to _____ . That movement _____ even today.

4. The idea that the earth's land masses were once just one large land mass is called _____ .

5. It took about _____ for the continents to look as they do today.

6. The idea of continental drift started from the study of the continent's _____ .

7. The theory of continental drift was first proposed by the scientist _____ .

8. Evidence from _____ , _____ , _____ and the shapes of _____ support the theory of continental drift.

MATCHING

Match each term in Column A with its description in Column B. Write the correct letter in the space provided.

Column A	Column B
_____ 1. fossils	a) move apart slowly
_____ 2. drift	b) large land mass
_____ 3. continent	c) "super continent"
_____ 4. theory of continental drift	d) traces of living things
_____ 5. Pangaea	e) supported by most scientists

Figure E *Mesosaurus*

Alfred Wegener studied the fossils of Mesosaurus [meh-soh-SAWR-us]. Mesosaurus fossils were found in Africa and in South America. Mesosaurus was a fresh-water animal. Wegener wondered how it could swim across the salty Atlantic Ocean. He concluded that Mesosaurus must have lived on one land mass. When the land mass broke apart, some of the animals were trapped on each part.

TRY IT YOURSELF

• Trace the continents shown on the map in Figure C.

• Glue your tracing onto a sheet of construction paper.

• Carefully cut out the continents. You should have seven.

• Arrange the pieces to form Pangaea.

• Glue the model of Pangaea onto another piece of construction paper.

Place the drawings of the way the earth looked in the correct order based upon continental drift. Write the number of years ago in the space provided. Use these labels: **250 million years ago, 150 million years ago, 100 million years ago, 50 million years ago, present.**

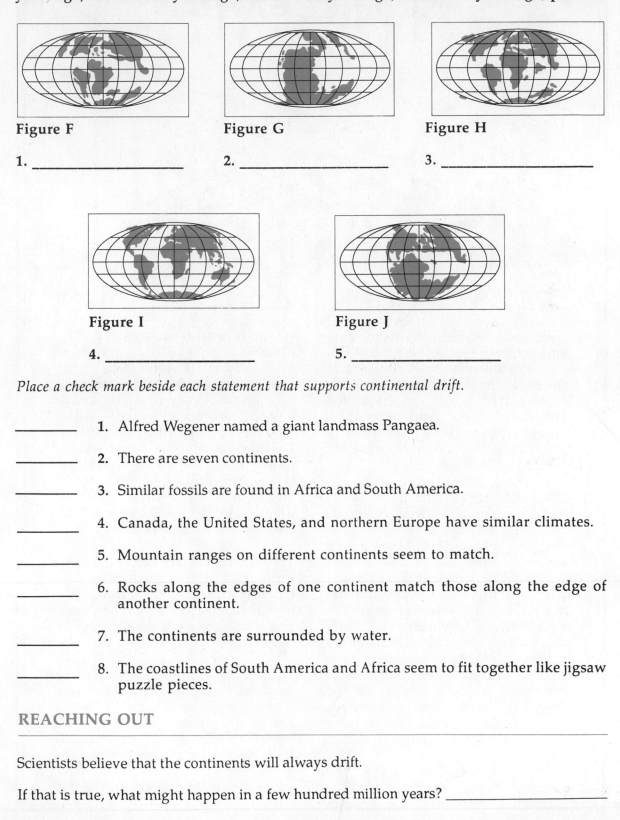

Figure F

1. _____

Figure G

2. _____

Figure H

3. _____

Figure I

4. _____

Figure J

5. _____

Place a check mark beside each statement that supports continental drift.

_____ 1. Alfred Wegener named a giant landmass Pangaea.

_____ 2. There are seven continents.

_____ 3. Similar fossils are found in Africa and South America.

_____ 4. Canada, the United States, and northern Europe have similar climates.

_____ 5. Mountain ranges on different continents seem to match.

_____ 6. Rocks along the edges of one continent match those along the edge of another continent.

_____ 7. The continents are surrounded by water.

_____ 8. The coastlines of South America and Africa seem to fit together like jigsaw puzzle pieces.

REACHING OUT

Scientists believe that the continents will always drift.

If that is true, what might happen in a few hundred million years? _____

_____

SCIENCE *EXTRA*

The Chunnel

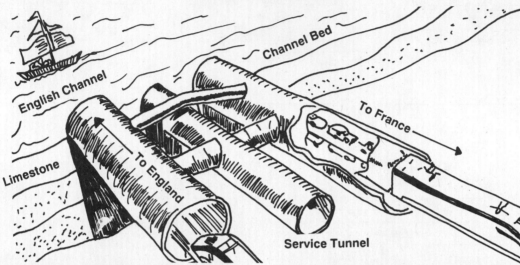

Geologists believe that Great Britain was once connected to the rest of Europe by a low lying plain. However, at the end of the last ice age, about seven thousand years ago, glaciers melted and flooded this plain. Since then, Great Britain has been reachable only by crossing the often stormy waters of the English channel.

What nature had done, human technology has undone. On December 1, 1991, Graham Fagg of Dover, England and Philippe Cozette of Calais, France became the first two people to travel under the English Channel. Fagg was a member of a team of engineers that started digging a tunnel under the Channel from Great Britain. Cozette was part of a similar team of engineers that started digging under the Channel from France. The two tunnels were connected on December '1, 1991 as Fagg and Cozette used jackhammers to knock out the last foot of limestone that had separated the two tunnels.

When it is completed in 1993, the Channel Tunnel, also known as the "Chunnel," will be the world's long-est underwater passageway. The Chunnel actually will consist of three tunnels. Two of the tunnels will be for rail trains. One of the train tunnels will be for travel from Great Britain to France. The other train tunnel will be for travel from France to Great Britain. The third tunnel will be a maintenance tunnel. It will run between the other two tunnels and will be connected to the two train tunnels in several hundred places. This will allow service crews to reach trouble spots quickly.

The trains will carry passengers and cargo, including automobiles. The crossing will take only thirty-five minutes compared to the ninety minutes it takes to cross the Channel by ferry boat.

The idea of digging a tunnel under the English Channel is not new. The idea was first considered in the 1700s and has been proposed countless times since then. However, it was not until the 1980s that there was the technology and desire to successfully carry out the project, and reunite a continent.

What is the theory of plate tectonics?

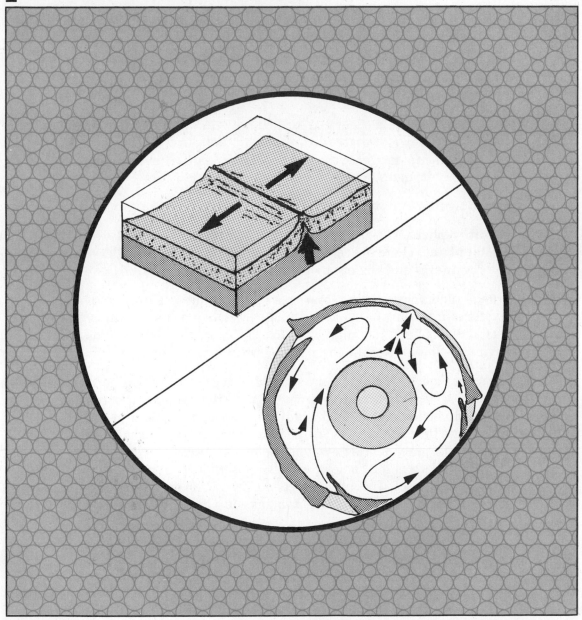

convection [kuhn-VEK-shun] **currents**: movement of a gas or liquid caused by
     changes in temperature
crustal plates: large pieces of the solid part of the earth
mid-ocean ridge: underwater mountain chain
sea-floor spreading: process that forms new sea-floor
theory of plate tectonics [tek-TAHN-iks]: theory that states the earth's crust is
     broken into pieces that float on the lower mantle

LESSON 21 | What is the theory of plate tectonics?

For many years, most geologists did not accept the theory of continental drift. The main reason was that it did not explain <u>why</u> or <u>how</u> the continents drifted apart.

Today, scientists have a theory to explain how the continents are drifting apart. The **theory of plate tectonics** [tek-TAHN-ics] states how and why the continents move. It also explains how natural events such as earthquakes, volcanoes, and mountain building occur.

There are two main points of the theory of plate tectonics:

- The lithosphere is the solid layer of the earth. It is broken up into **crustal plates**. There are seven main plates and several smaller ones. The continents and the ocean floor rest upon the plates.

- Crustal plates float on the lower part of the mantle. This part of the mantle is made up of solid rock that flows like a thick liquid. The crustal plates float like rafts on a lake. The continents and oceans are carried on the plates like the passengers on a raft.

What causes plate tectonics? Scientists think that giant **convection** [kuhn-VEK-shun] **currents** in the earth's mantle cause the movement of crustal plates. A convection current is the movement of a gas or a liquid caused by differences in temperature. The mantle rock close to the center of the earth is hot. The rock farther away is cooler. The hot rock rises and the cooler rock sinks. As the cooler rock gets closer to the earth's center, it heats up. Then it rises. This process repeats itself in an endless cycle. The crustal plates are carried along like packages on a moving conveyor belt.

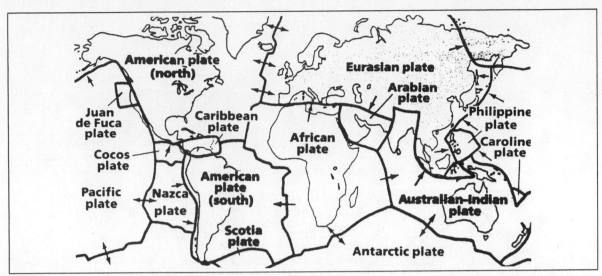

Figure A

Use Figure A and the reading material to answer the questions below.

1. What is the lithosphere? _____

_____

2. What is the lithosphere broken into? _____

3. How many major crustal plates are there? _____

4. Name 5 crustal plates. _____

_____

5. What is the largest crustal plate? _____

6. What things rest upon crustal plates? _____

_____

7. On what layer do the crustal plates float? _____

_____

8. Describe the lower part of the mantle. _____

_____

CONVECTIONS CURRENTS

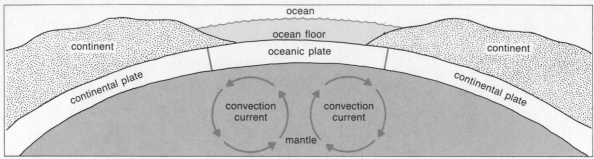

Figure B *Convention current movement in the mantle.*

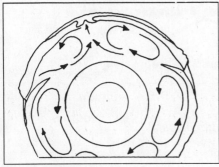

Figure C

Figure C shows how some scientists believe convection currents cause the crustal plates to move. The mantle rock near the earth's core is hot. The hot mantle rock rises. The cooler mantle rock sinks closer to the core and gets heated up. This cycle repeats over and over. When the heated rock rises, it causes the crustal plates to move.

MULTIPLE CHOICE

In the space provided, write the letter of the word that best completes each statement.

_____ 1. A convection current is caused by differences in

    a) temperature.   **b)** mass.

    c) air pressure.   **d)** color.

_____ 2. Scientists think that the movement of crustal plates is caused by

    a) conveyor belts.   **b)** pressure in the earths core.

    c) the core.   **d)** convection currents.

_____ 3. The mantle rock close to the center of the earth is

    a) cold.   **b)** hot.

    c) frozen.   **d)** sinking.

_____ 4. The center of the earth is called the

    a) crust.   **b)** mantle.

    c) core.   **d)** lithosphere.

_____ 5. If you added cold water to a container of hot water, the cold water would

    a) rise.   **b)** get colder.

    c) sink.   **d)** stay on top.

The crustal plates move in different ways.

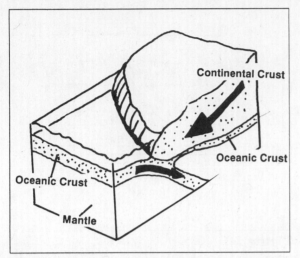

Figure D *Some plates are moving toward each other. At these places, two plates hit each other. Sometimes the oceanic crust is pushed under the continents crust.*

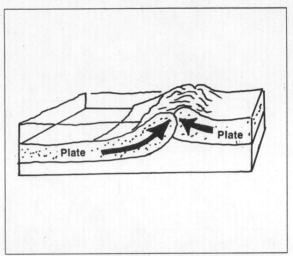

Figure E *Sometimes two plates carrying continents crumple upward when plates collide.*

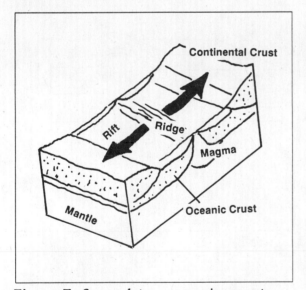

Figure F *Some plates are moving apart.*

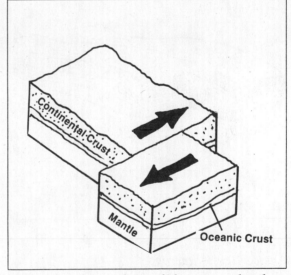

Figure G *Some plates slide past each other.*

• The movement of crustal plates causes changes on the earth's surface.

• In some areas where crustal plates slide past each other, the movement causes earthquakes.

• When oceanic crust is pushed down under continental crust, the continental crust crumples. It is pushed upward to form new mountains.

• When two crustal plates carrying continents collide, the continents buckle upward and form mountains. The Himalaya mountains were formed in this way when the plate carrying India collided with the Eurasian plate.

On each diagram, draw arrows to show the different ways in which crustal plates move.

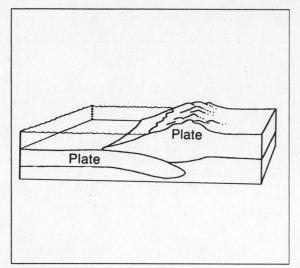

Figure H

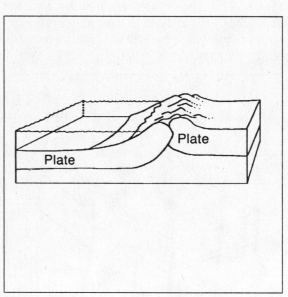

Figure I

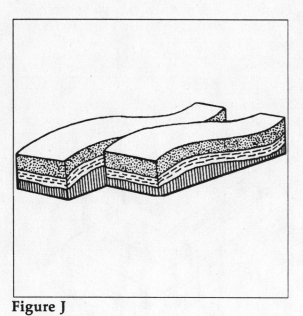

Figure J

Figure K

Answer the following.

5. The movement of crustal plates sliding past each other causes _____ .

   earthquakes, mountain building

6. Sometimes when two plates collide _____ crust is pushed down under

   continental, oceanic

   the _____ crust.

   continental, crustal

7. When this happens _____ occurs.

   earthquakes, mountain building

8. When two plates carrying continents collide, the continents buckle_____ .

   upward, downward

9. This causes _____ .

   an earthquake, mountain building

134

SEA-FLOOR SPREADING

You may think that the ocean floor is flat. Does it surprise you that some of the largest mountain ranges and tallest mountains are under the ocean? They are! The mountain chain under the ocean is called the **mid-ocean ridge**.

At the mid-ocean ridge, magma was rising through the crust. As the magma cooled, it hardened and formed new crust on both sides of the ridge. The sea-floor was spreading apart at the ridges. New oceanic crust was being formed, and pushed out the older crust next to it. Older crust is pushed into deep ocean valleys. Scientists call this process **sea-floor spreading**. Sea-floor spreading supports plate tectonics.

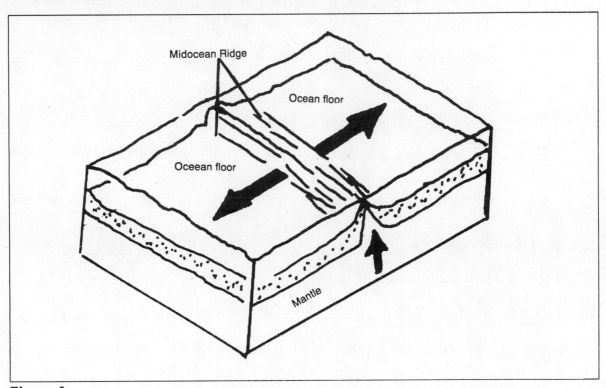

Figure L

TRUE OR FALSE

In the space provided, write "true" if the sentence is true. Write "false" if the sentence is false.

_____ 1. Mountains are found only on the continents.

_____ 2. The underwater mountain chain is called the mid-ocean ridge.

_____ 3. New oceanic crust is formed at the mid-ocean ridge.

_____ 4. Oceanic crust near a mid-ocean ridge is older than crust far away.

_____ 5. Sea-floor spreading supports plate tectonics.

FILL IN THE BLANK

Complete each statement using a term or terms from the list below. Write your answers in the spaces provided.

collide	flows	plate tectonics
continents	mantle	rises
convection currents	move	sinks
crustal plates	ocean floor	solid

1. The idea that explains how and why continents drift is called the theory of _____.

2. The lithosphere is made up of large moving sections called _____.

3. The lithosphere is _____.

4. Crustal plates float on the lower layer of the _____.

5. Giant _____ in the earth's mantle cause the crustal plates to move.

6. The lower layer of the mantle is solid rock that _____ like a thick liquid.

7. Crustal plates carry the _____ and _____.

8. Mountains may form where plates _____.

9. Hot rock in the mantle _____ while cooler rock _____.

10. Scientists believe that the continents, along with the ocean floor will continue to _____.

REACHING OUT

Upon which plate is each of the following places located? Check an atlas or encyclopedia and Figure A.

	Plate		**Plate**
1. Canada	_____	6. Brazil	_____
2. France	_____	7. Nigeria	_____
3. Hawaii	_____	8. Australia	_____
4. Russia	_____	9. Panama	_____
5. South Pole	_____	10. YOU!	_____

136

What are plains and plateaus?

22

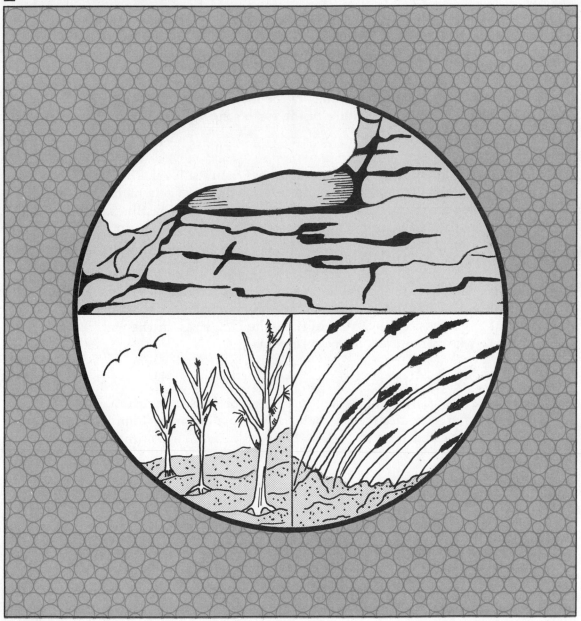

landform: physical feature of the earth's surface
plain: large flat area not much higher than sea level
plateau [pla-TOH]: large flat region with higher elevation than a plain

LESSON 22 | What are plains and plateaus?

Imagine that you are flying across the United States. What surface features would you see? You would probably see mountains, small swift streams, and dense forests. You also would see large flat areas, **plains** and **plateaus**

Mountains, plains and plateaus are the main continental **landforms**. A landform is a physical feature of the earth's surface.

PLAINS

A plain is a large flat area not much higher than sea level. There are two kinds of plains, coastal plains and interior plains. Their names tell us where they are found. Coastal plains are found along coastlines. Interior plains are located inland. All plains slope, but very gently, so gently in fact, that most plains seem to be as even as a bowling alley. Some plains also have gentle rolling hills.

Plains are formed in several ways. One way is through erosion. Uneven elevated land is worn down. Another way is through deposition. Sediments are deposited in water. In time, the land rises, or the water level drops. A large flat area, or plain remains.

PLATEAUS

A plateau is a large flat region, just like a plain is. However, plateaus have higher elevations than plains. Most plateaus are found inland. Some are located near the ocean. Plateaus near the ocean usually end with a cliff.

Many plateaus have canyons. A canyon is a steep-sided valley carved out by steam erosion. One of the most well-known canyons is the Grand Canyon. It is located in the southwest United States.

How do plateaus form? Large areas of the earth's crust are moved upward. Or, some plateaus are formed by lava. The lava cools and hardens, forming a large raised area.

LANDFORMS OF THE UNITED STATES

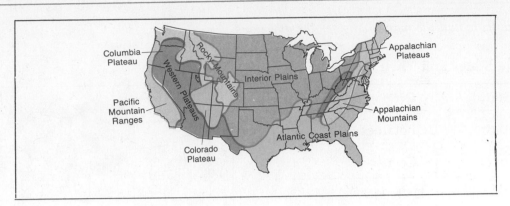

Figure A

Study Figure A then answer the questions below.

1. Which is the largest landform region in the United States? _____

2. In what landform region do you live? _____

3. What two landforms are found in the western United States? _____

   _____

Figure B *The majestic and breathtaking Grand Canyon!*

4. Upon what kind of landform is the Grand Canyon? _____

   _____

5. What formed the Grand Canyon? (Look back at Lesson 15)

   _____

   _____

Figure C

The interior plains of the United States, or the Great Plains as it often is called, has very fertile soil. The soil is very good for farming. This region produces more wheat and corn than any other region of the world.

MORE ABOUT THE GREAT PLAINS

Use the table and the map to answer the questions.

Some States and Their Crops

State	Crop
Idaho	Potatoes
Iowa	Corn
Kansas	Wheat
Wisconsin	Alfalfa

Figure D

1. How many states make up the Great Plains? _____

2. Name five states that are part of the great Plains? _____

_____

3. Name four crops that are grown in the Great Plains. _____

_____

4. The twelve states in the Great Plains are nicknamed the "breadbasket" of the world.

    Why do you think these states were given this name? _____

_____

MATCHING

Match each term in Column A with its description in Column B. Write the correct letter in the space provided.

Column A

_____ 1. flat area near a coastline that is not far above sea level

_____ 2. steep-sided valley formed by a river

_____ 3. flat area located inland that has a low elevation

_____ 4. large, flat area with high elevation

_____ 5. physical feature of the earth's surface

Column B

a) landform

b) coastal plain

c) interior plain

d) plateau

e) canyon

140

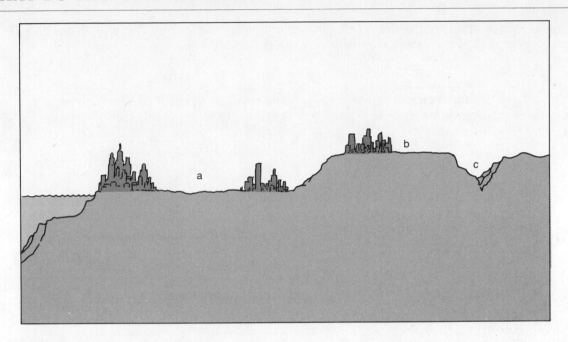

Figure E

Identify features shown on this cross-section.

a. _____   b. _____   c. _____

TRUE OR FALSE

In the space provided, write "true" if the sentence is true. Write "false" if the sentence is false.

_____ 1. All plains slope very gently.

_____ 2. Lava formed some plains.

_____ 3. Many plateaus have canyons.

_____ 4. The Great Plains have very fertile soil.

_____ 5. The Grand Canyon was formed by lava.

_____ 6. Plains are higher than plateaus.

_____ 7. Some plains have rolling hills.

_____ 8. The western United States has many plains.

_____ 9. Most plateaus are found inland.

_____ 10. A plain is not much higher than sea level.

FILL IN THE BLANK

Complete each statement using a term or terms from the list below. Write your answers in the spaces provided. Some words may be used more than once.

mountains	inland	flat
landforms	sea level	higher
canyons	cliff	plateaus
erosion	plains	deposition
lava		

1. The physical characteristics of the earth's surface are called _____.

2. The three basic continental landforms are _____, _____, and _____.

3. A plain is a large _____ area not far above _____.

4. A plain may be formed either by _____ or by _____.

5. Plateaus near the ocean usually end with a _____.

6. Plateaus are much _____ in elevation than plains.

7. Some plateaus were formed from _____ that cooled and hardened.

8. A canyon is carved out by stream _____.

9. Most plateaus are located _____.

10. Many plateaus have steep-sided valleys called _____.

WORD SCRAMBLE

Below are several scrambled words you have used in this Lesson. Unscramble the words and write your answers in the spaces provided.

1. MLRAONFD _____

2. SPNAIL _____

3. SCNAONY _____

4. TLFA _____

5. TULAPEA _____

What are mountains?

23

LESSON 23 | What are mountains?

Everybody knows what a mountain is. It is a section of land that is much higher than the land around it. To be classified as a mountain the top of a hill or mound of land must be at least 600 meters higher than the surrounding land.

Mountains can be beautiful to see. Some mountains are very high, with snow-capped peaks. Such mountains are usually rocky and have sharp, jagged edges. Other mountains are lower. They are more rounded and are covered with trees.

Mountains can be described in three stages: <u>young</u>, <u>mature</u>, and <u>old</u>. A young mountain has a steep slope. Its peaks are sharp and jagged. The valleys in young mountains are narrow.

As a mountain becomes mature, its peaks are worn down by weathering. The peaks become more rounded. The slopes become less steep.

As a mountain becomes old, its peaks become almost flat. There are no jagged peaks. An old mountain looks like rolling hills. The valleys in old mountains are wide.

MOUNTAIN SYSTEMS

Most mountains do not stand alone. They are part of a group of mountains. A group of mountains with the same shape and structure is called a <u>mountain range</u>. Groups of mountain ranges form <u>mountain systems</u>. Mountain systems make up <u>mountain belts</u>. There are only two main mountain belts.

Figure A *Mount St. Helens in Washington State is part of the Cascade mountain range.*

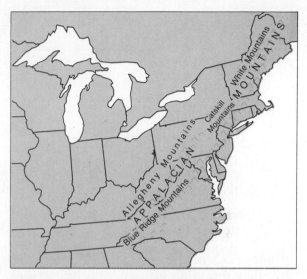

Figure B *The Appalachian mountain system is in the eastern United States. The Blue Ridge and Great Smokey mountain ranges are part of the Appalachian System.*

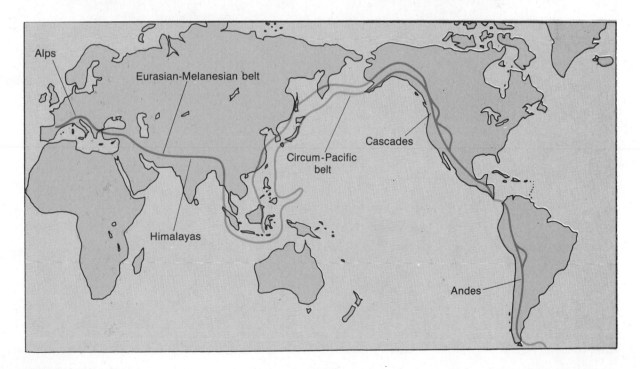

Figure C *The two major mountain belts are the Eurasian-Melanesian [yoo-RAY-zhen mel-uh-NEE-zhun] and the Circum-Pacific belt.*

COMPLETE THE CHART

Answer the questions by putting a "YES" or "NO" in the space provided.

Characterisitic	Young	Mature	Old
1. Wide valley			
2. Sharp, jagged peaks			
3. Gentle slope			
4. Elevation greater than 600 meters			
5. Narrow valleys			
6. Rounded peaks			
7. Almost flat peaks			
8. Looks like rolling hills			

WHAT DO THE PICTURES SHOW?

Figures D and E show two different stages of the same mountain. Figures F and G show another mountain at two different stages. Study the pictures and then identify the two stages of each mountain shown.

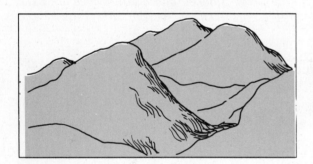

Figure D

9. old or young? _____

Figure E

10. mature or young? _____

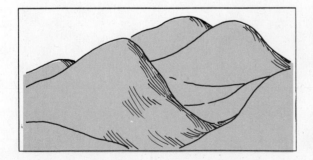

Figure F

11. mature or old? _____

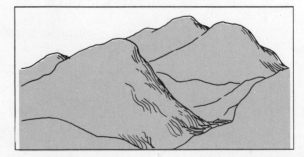

Figure G

12. mature or old? _____

MORE ABOUT MOUNTAINS

Use the map to answer the following questions.

1. Name the mountain ranges that make up the Appalachian mountain system.

   _____

   _____

2. Name the four states that the Allegheny mountains are found in.

   _____

   _____

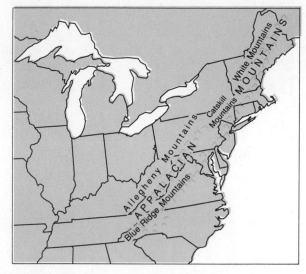

Figure H

TRUE OR FALSE

In the space provided, write "true" if the sentence is true. Write "false" if the sentence is false.

_____ 1. Mountains can be described in three stages.

_____ 2. All mountains have snow-capped peaks.

_____ 3. Most mountains stand alone.

_____ 4. There are three main mountain belts.

_____ 5. The valleys in old mountains are narrow.

_____ 6. Groups of mountain ranges form mountain systems.

_____ 7. The peaks of a mountain are worn down by weathering.

_____ 8. Old mountains look like rolling hills.

_____ 9. All mountains are at least 600 meters high.

_____ 10. A young mountain has flat peaks.

WORD SEARCH

The list on the left contains words that you have used in this Lesson. Find and circle each word where it appears in the box. The spellings may go in any direction: up, down, left, right, or diagonally.

YOUNG

JAGGED

MOUNTAIN

RANGE

PEAK

BELTS

OLD

MATURE

SLOPE

VALLEYS

A	F	G	Y	O	U	N	G	G	E
C	M	M	D	S	U	E	F	P	M
J	M	O	G	H	V	P	W	A	S
A	S	L	U	O	K	O	P	E	E
G	N	D	L	N	A	L	S	G	R
G	B	B	E	L	T	S	N	L	U
E	O	M	O	P	E	A	K	O	T
D	L	G	G	A	R	M	I	R	A
N	P	E	A	C	L	D	V	N	M
L	G	V	A	L	L	E	Y	S	N

REACHING OUT

Researching: Find out the missing information to complete the chart below.

Three Famous Mountains

Name	Height (meters)	Country	Mountain Range
Mount McKinley		United States	
Mount Whitney	4418		Sierra Nevada
Mount Everest			

1. Which of the mountains is the highest? _____

2. Which mountain(s) are found in the United States? _____

_____

How are mountains formed?

24

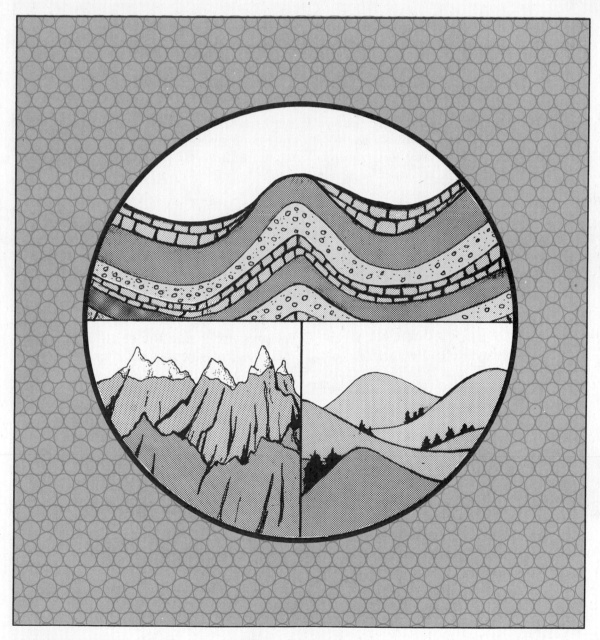

anticline [AN-tih-klyn]: upward fold
fault: break in the earth's crust along which movement has occured
fracture [FRAK-chur]: break in a rock
syncline [SIN-klyn]: downward fold

LESSON 24 | How are mountains formed?

The Himalayas, the Sierra Nevadas, and the Black Hills of South Dakota are all mountains. However, they are different kinds of mountains.

There are three different kinds of mountains: folded mountains, fault-block mountains, and domed mountains.

FOLDED MOUNTAINS   Usually, you think of rock as being very hard and brittle. You probably cannot imagine bending, or "folding," a rock. However, over very long periods of time (millions of years), pressure can cause thick layers of sedimentary rock to buckle and fold.

Layers of folded rock look something like waves. They have upward folds and downward folds. An upward fold is called an **anticline** [AN-tih-klyn]. A downward fold is called a **syncline** [SIN-klyn]. Folded mountains are anticlines that rise high above the land around them. Most folded mountains formed when the continents collided. The movements of the continents squeezed rock layers together. The Himalayas are folded mountains.

FAULT-BLOCK MOUNTAINS   Great pressure inside the earth does not always fold the earth's crust. Sometimes pressure breaks rocks. A break in a rock is called a **fracture** [FRAK-chur]. If rocks on either side of a fracture move, the break is called a **fault**.

The movement of rocks along a fault is called faulting. Sometimes faulting lifts large blocks of the earth's crust. If the blocks are pushed up enough, a fault-block mountain is formed. The Sierra Nevadas are fault-block mountains.

DOME MOUNTAINS   Some mountains form when magma tries to rise through the crust. However, in some places, the rock above the magma is extra strong. The magma pushes, but it cannot force its way to the surface. As pressure builds, the magma bulges. This bulge forces the rock above it to bulge also. The land on the surface rises. A domed mountain is formed. Domed mountains are oval or round. The Black Hills are domed mountains.

HOW CAN WE SHOW FOLDING?

You can use a stack of colored paper to show how sedimentary rock can be folded. First, arrange the stack in layers of different colored paper. (Figure A, top).

Next, slowly but firmly push both ends of the stack of paper toward the center (Figure A, bottom)

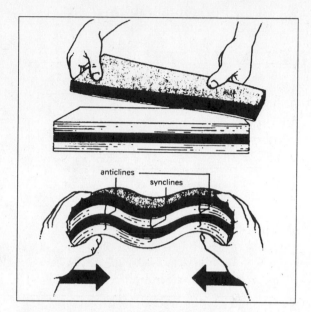

1. What do the different colored layers

   of paper stand for? _____

2. What happens to the layers as the

   pressure builds up on the ends of the

   stack? _____

Figure A

WHAT DOES THE DIAGRAM SHOW?

The diagram below shows folded rock layers. Study the diagram. Then answer the questions.

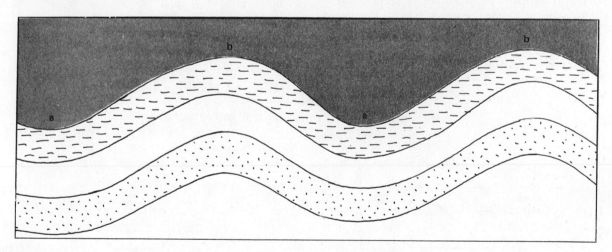

Figure B

1. The upfolds are lettered _____ .   2. The downfolds are lettered _____ .

3. The anticlines are lettered _____ .   4. The synclines are lettered _____ .

5. Moving plates can squeeze rock layers together into mountains. The mountains are

   called _____ mountains.

horizontal faulting
Side-to-side

horizontal faulting
Side-to-side

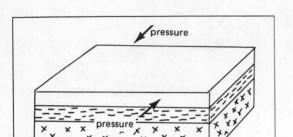

Figure C

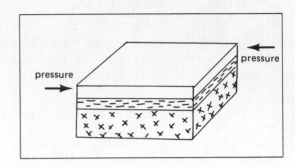

Figure D

- Forces inside the earth press against rocks.

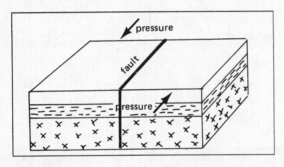

Figure E

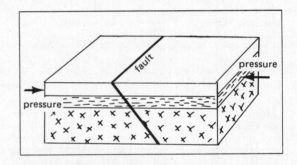

Figure F

- Sometimes the pressure is too great.
- The rock cracks.
- But the split parts do not move yet.

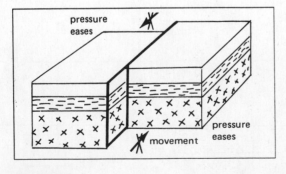

Figure G

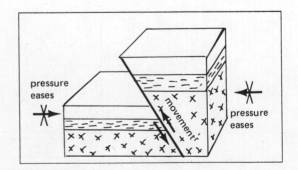

Figure H

- More pressure builds
- Then the pressure eases.
- Suddenly, the blocks move in opposite directions.

WHAT DOES THE PICTURE SHOW?

The rocks in this diagram have faulted. One block has moved up. The other block has moved down. Study the diagram of the layers carefully, then answer the questions.

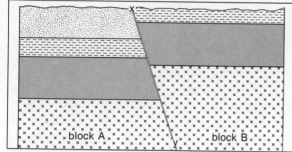

Figure I

1. Block A has moved _____ .

2. Block B has moved _____ .

3. What is line XY called? _____

4. The movement of rocks along a

   fault is called _____ .

5. This is an example of _____

   faulting.

HOW A DOMED MOUNTAIN IS FORMED

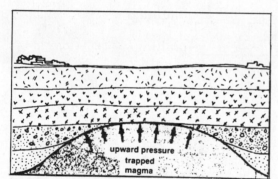

Figure J *Trapped magma builds strong upward pressure.*

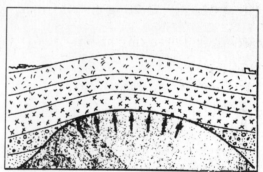

Figure K *The pressure bulges the land above it.*

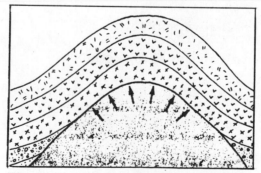

Figure L *A great domed mountain is formed.*

FILL IN THE BLANK

Complete each statement using a term or terms from the list below. Write your answers in the spaces provided. Some words may be used more than once.

horzontal   bulge   fault-block vertical
dome   folded   syncline   faulting
anticline

1.   The three kinds of mountains are _____ , _____ and

  _____ .

2.   The movement of rock along a fault is called _____ .

3.   The force of trapped magma can make the land above it _____ .

4.   A upfold in rock is called an _____ .

5.   Land pushed up high by trapped magma forms a _____ mountain.

6.   A downfold in rock is called a _____ .

7.   Up-and-down faulting also is called _____ faulting.

8.   Side-to-side faulting also is called _____ faulting.

TRUE OR FALSE

In the space provided, write "true" if the sentence is true. Write "false" if the sentence is false.

_____ 1.   Magma always reaches the earth's surface.

_____ 2.   Pressure can split rocks.

_____ 3.   Pressure will always fold rock.

_____ 4.   Pressure will always split a rock.

_____ 5.   Most folded mountains formed when the continents collided.

_____ 6.   Domed mountains are oval or round.

_____ 7.   Faulting builds dome mountains.

What is a contour map? 25

contour [KON-toor] **map**: a map that shows the elevation and depression of the land
depressions: distance of a point on the earth below sea level
elevation [el-uh-VAY-shun]: distance of a point on the earth above sea level
sea level: average level of the water in the oceans

LESSON 25 | What is a contour map?

There are many different kinds of maps. The maps we use most often are surface maps. A surface map is a drawing. It shows all or part of the earth's surface.

There is one problem with a surface map. It is flat, but, the earth's surface is not all flat. It has hills and mountains, plateaus, valleys, and oceans.

The different parts of the earth's surface are at different heights, or **elevations**. The elevation of the ocean's surface is zero. This is called **sea level**. The rest of the earth's surface is measured from sea level. So, elevation is measured in meters or feet above (or below) sea level.

How can a flat map show elevation? Or changes in elevation? Some maps use color. Others use shading. However, such maps give only a general idea about the surface.

There is a special kind of map, called a **contour** (KON-toor) **map**. "Contour" means shape. A contour map shows the true shape of the land. It also shows elevations and changes in elevation.

A contour map shows shape and elevation by means of contour lines. <u>A contour line is a line that connects points that are at the same elevation.</u>

- Every point on a given contour line is at the same elevation.

- Several contour lines make up a contour map.

- The <u>difference in elevation between two neighboring contour lines is called the contour interval of the map</u>.

- Contour lines can show how much the land slopes.

Contour lines that are <u>far apart</u> indicate that the land is fairly flat, or has a <u>gentle</u> slope.

Contour lines that are <u>close together</u> show that the land is hilly, or has a <u>steep</u> slope.

Hilltops are enclosed by small contour lines. The exact elevation of a hilltop is shown by a small triangle beside the true elevation of the hill. For example, ▲ 118 means that elevation of the peak is 118 meters.

Look at the Figures A and B.

Figure A

Figure B

Figure **A** shows an island.

Figure **B** shows a contour map of this island.

Answer the questions below by studying the contour map.

1. How long is this island? _____.

2. How wide is this island? _____.

3. This island starts at sea level. How do you know? (Look only at the contour map.)

   _____.

4. What is the contour interval of this map? _____.

5. Which side of the island has the steepest slope? _____.
   north, south, east, west

6. How do you know? _____.

7. Which side of the island has the gentlest slope? _____.
   north, south, east, west

8. How do you know? _____.

9. How high is the peak of this island? _____.

Compare the drawing of the island with the contour map.

12. Which one gives more information? _____.

13. Which one is more accurate? _____.

14. Which one is more useful? _____.

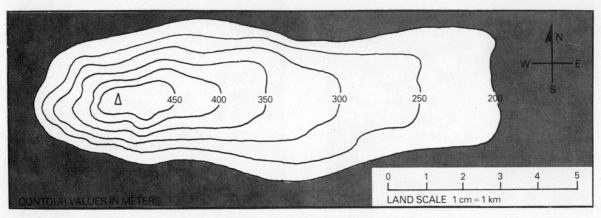

Figure C

Let's try another. By compass direction...

1. The _____ side of this landform has the steepest slope.

2. The _____ side of this landform has the gentlest slope.

3. The contour interval of this map is _____ meters.

4. The lowest elevation shown is _____ meters.

5. Which of these heights could be the <u>exact</u> elevation of the peak?

    a) 520 meters   **b)** 420 meters **c)** 475 meters

SOMETHING EXTRA

You can learn more from a contour map than just the shape and slope of the land. Contour maps also tell you something about streams. And about "dips," or **depressions**, in the land.

STREAMS

The head of a stream is the place where it starts. The place where it ends, in a lake or ocean is called the mouth. Look at Figure D. Can you find a stream?

<u>What letter is at</u>

1. the head of the stream? _____

2. the mouth of the stream? _____

3. Everyone knows that water flows _____.
   <small>uphill, downhill</small>

4. In other words, water flows from a _____ elevation to a _____
   <small>higher, lower</small>   <small>higher, lower</small>
   elevation.

5. At a stream, contour lines seem to form "arrows." Each "arrow" points...

   toward the _____ of the stream, _____ , _____ the
   <small>head, mouth</small>   <small>upstream, downstream</small>   <small>toward, away from</small>
   direction of flow.

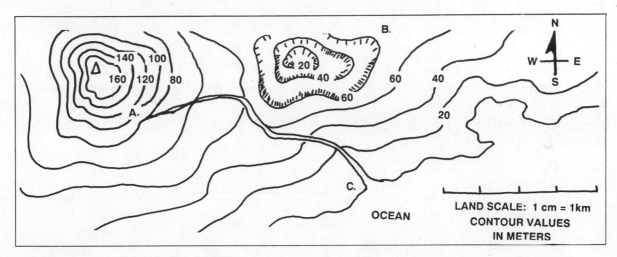

Figure D

DEPRESSIONS

Sometimes a bowl-like dip or depression occurs on a fairly flat surface. These are shown by special contour lines called depression contours. A depression contour is shaded, or hachured, on one side, like this |||||||||||||||||||| . The hachures point down into the depression.

Depression contours are just like regular contour lines. They show the shape of the depression. They also show the slope of the sides of the depression.

Look at the depression beside letter **B** on the map above.

1. The elevation at the top of the depression is _____ meters.

2. The _____ side of the depression has the steepest slope.
   <small>north,. south, east, west</small>

3. Which of these could be the exact elevation at the bottom of the depression?

   a) 40 meters   **b)** 20 meters   **c)** 10 meters

159

FILL IN THE BLANK

Complete each statement using a term or terms from the list below. Write your answers in the spaces provided.

steep   contour map   depression contours
contour lines   gentle   elevation
zero (0)   contour interval   hachures
sea level

1. A map that accurately shows the shape and changing elevations of the land is called

    a _____.

2. The height of a location is called its _____.

3. Contour maps use _____ to show shape and elevation.

4. The difference in elevation between two neighboring contour lines is called the

    _____.

5. All elevations are measured from _____.

6. The number value of sea level is _____.

7. Contour lines that are close together indicate a _____ slope.

8. Contour lines that are far apart indicate a _____ slope.

9. Dips in fairly flat surface shown by _____.

10. The shading marks on a depression contour are called _____.

MATCHING

Match each term in Column A with its description in Column B. Write the correct letter in the space provided.

Column A	Column B
_____ 1. depression contours	a) height above sea level
_____ 2. elevation	b) show dips in a flat surface
_____ 3. contour interval	c) has zero elevation
_____ 4. mouth	d) difference between two neighboring contour lines
_____ 5. sea level	e) where a stream ends

160

What are earthquakes?

earthquakes: sudden, strong movements of the earth's crust
epicenter [EP-ih-sen-ter]: place on the surface of the earth directly above the focus
focus [FOH-kus]: place inside the earth where an earthquake starts
seismic [SYZ-mik]: **waves:** earthquake waves

LESSON 26 | What are earthquakes?

It was February 4, 1976, in Guatemala City. The time was 3 a.m. People were asleep. Suddenly the ground began to shake. It shook with great force. Walls tumbled, roofs caved in, whole buildings split in half, hillsides collapsed.

The shaking lasted only 39 seconds. In that short time, 26,000 people died in the city and countryside. Another 60,000 people were injured. Hundreds of thousands were left without homes.

An earthquake had struck in Guatemala. What is an earthquake? What causes earthquakes?

You have learned that faulting can build mountains. Faulting also causes earthquakes. When blocks of the earth's crust move, the movement shakes the earth. Sudden, strong movements of the earth's crust are called **earthquakes.**

Earthquakes begin deep inside the earth. The place where an earthquake starts is the **focus** [FOH-kus]. The place on the surface of the earth directly above the focus is called the **epicenter** [EP-ih-sen-ter]. The surface of the earth shakes hardest at the epicenter.

When rocks move, they release energy. The energy is in the form of waves—called **seismic** [SYZ-mik] **waves** or earthquake waves. These waves move out from the focus in all directions. Think of throwing a pebble into a pond. Where the pebble hits the water, you see waves move outward in all directions. Earthquake waves move out from the focus in the same way.

MEASURING EARTHQUAKES

A <u>seismograph</u> [SIZE-muh-graf] is an instrument that measures the strength of earthquakes. It makes a record of the movements of the earth's crust on a piece of paper. The record is called a seismogram [SIZE-muh-gram]. It looks like wavy lines. The higher the wavy lines, the stronger the earthquake. There are more than 500 seismograph stations. They are spread over every continent.

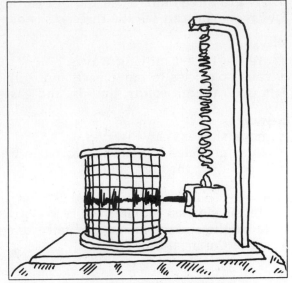

Figure A

Study Figures C and D and then answer the questions.

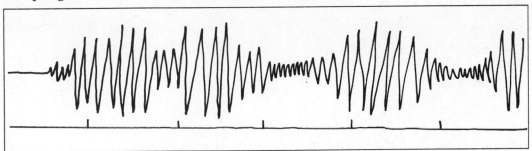

Figure B

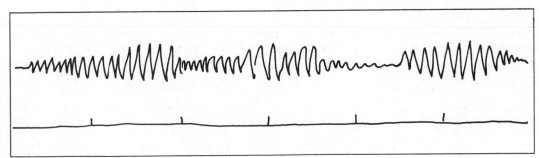

Figure C

1. What are Figures B and C? _____

2. Which Figure shows the stronger earthquake? _____

3. What instrument was used to get Figures B and C? _____

SEISMIC WAVES

There are three kinds of seismic, or earthquake waves. They are P-waves, S-waves, and L-waves. You can see the three kinds of waves in Figure D.

P-waves
- are the fastest moving waves.
- cause particles to move back and forth in place.
- move through solids, liquids, and gases.

S-waves
- move slower than P-waves.
- cause particles in materials to move from side to side.
- travel only through solids.

L-waves
- are the slowest moving waves.
- cause the surface to rise and fall like ocean waves.
- cause the most damage.

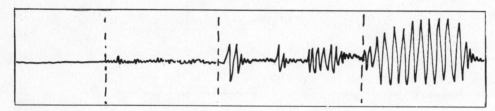

Figure D

COMPLETE THE CHART

Answer the questions by putting a "YES" or "NO" in the space provided.

Characteristics	P-waves	S-waves	L-waves
1. Travel through gases?			
2. Travel through liquids?			
3. Travel through solids?			
4. Fastest Waves?			
5. Surface waves?			
6. Slowest waves?			
7. Cause particles to move back and forth in place?			
8. Cause particles to move from side to side?			
9. Cause the most damage?			
10. Cause the surface to rise and fall like ocean waves?			

In 1935, Charles Richter [RIK-ter] developed a scale to measure the energy released by earthquakes. It is called the Richter scale.

On the Richter scale, an earthquake is given a number between 1 and 9. The higher the number is, the stronger the earthquake.

An earthquake measuring 7 or more can cause a lot of damage. Earthquakes that measure 2.5 or less on the scale usually are not felt by people.

The numbers below are numbers from the Richter Scale. Place the numbers in order from the weakest earthquake (a) to the strongest earthquake (j).

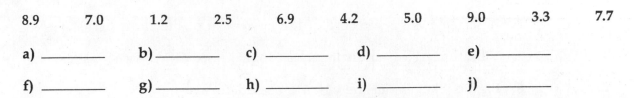

8.9   7.0   1.2   2.5   6.9   4.2   5.0   9.0   3.3   7.7

a) _____   b) _____   c) _____   d) _____   e) _____

f) _____   g) _____   h) _____   i) _____   j) _____

Figure E   *Earthquakes can happen in rocks under the ocean. The shaking of the rocks can set off huge tidal waves. When a tidal wave hits land, it can cause alot of damage.*

TRUE OR FALSE

In the space provided, write "true" if the sentence is true. Write "false" if the sentence is false.

_____ 1. An instrument that detects and measures earthquakes is a seismic wave.

_____ 2. The place inside the earth where an earthquake starts is called the focus.

_____ 3. Most earthquakes are caused by folding.

_____ 4. The place on the earth's crust directly above the place where an earthquake starts is called the focus.

_____ 5. An earthquake measuring less than 2.5 on the Richter Scale can cause a lot of damage.

_____ 6. A seismogram is a record of the movement of the earth's crust.

_____ 7. Vibrations released during an earthquake are called focus waves.

_____ 8. Earthquakes under the ocean cause tidal waves.

_____ 9. The higher the lines on a seismogram, the weaker the earthquake.

_____ 10. During an earthquake, the earth's surface shakes hardest at the epicenter.

NOW TRY THIS

Use the listed terms to label the diagrams. Write your answers in the provided spaces.

epicenter   focus   seismograph   seismogram   seismic waves

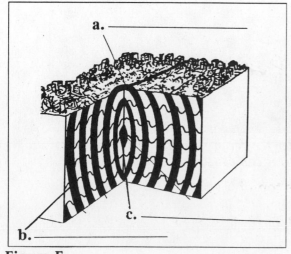

Figure F

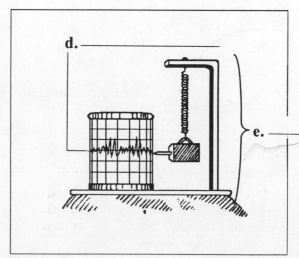

Figure G

What are volcanoes?

27

crater [KRAY-tur]:   funnel shaped pit at the top of a volcanic cone
vent: opening from which lava flows
volcano [vahl-KAY-noh]:   vent and the pile of volcanic material around the vent

LESSON 27 | What are volcanoes?

On May 18, 1980, Mount St. Helens in Washington State blew its top. The eruption sent ash high into the air. The blast caused great damage all around the mountain. Forests were destroyed. Rivers were blocked with mud, ash, and fallen trees. All plant and animal life were killed. Mount St. Helens is a volcanic mountain.

Most people call volcanic mountains **volcanoes** [vahl-KAY-nohs]. Volcanoes form in places where magma forces its way to the earth's surface. Once it reaches the earth's surface, magma is called lava. At the surface, lava cools and hardens. You may remember that it forms igneous rock.

The opening from which lava flows is called a **vent.** Dust, ash, and rock particles also are thrown out of a vent. A volcano is made up of the vent and the volcanic cone. The volcanic cone is the pile of lava, dust, ash, and rock around the vent. At the top of a volcano there maybe a funnel-shaped pit. It is called a **crater** [KRAY-tur]. A crater forms when material is blown out of the vent.

Volcanic eruptions may be quiet or explosive. During a quiet eruption, lava flows gently to the surface. It spreads out and forms a large mountain. The slopes are gentle. This kind of volcano is called a shield cone.

During explosive eruptions, lava, boulders, ashes, dust, and gases are sent high into the air. Explosive eruptions occur when magma inside the earth is under great pressure. The magma "explodes" to the surface. Volcanoes formed by explosive eruptions have steep sides and narrow bases. They are called cinder cones.

Between eruptions, a volcano is said to be "sleeping" or dormant.

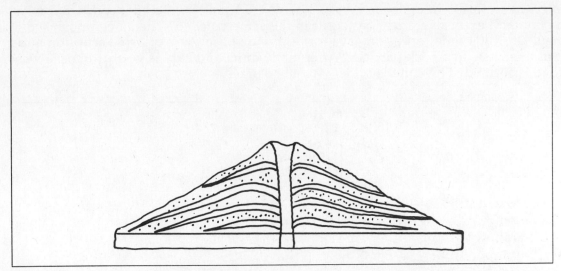

Figure A *A quiet eruption.*

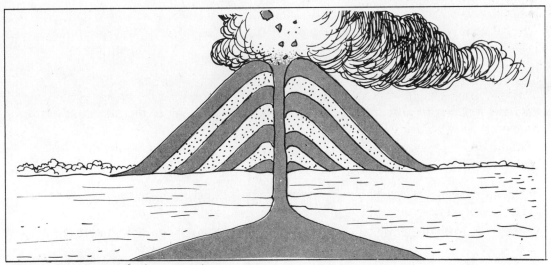

Figure B *An explosive eruption.*

1. The sides of a volcano formed by a quiet eruption are _____.
   <small>steep, gentle</small>

2. The sides of a volcano formed by an explosive eruption are _____.
   <small>steep, gentle</small>

3. Which has a wider base, a volcano formed by a quiet or an explosive eruption?

   _____

4. Which is a shield cone? _____
   <small>A, B</small>

5. Which is a cinder cone? _____
   <small>A, B</small>

169

MORE ABOUT VOLCANOES

A quiet eruption forms shield cones. An explosive eruption forms cinder cones. But what if both quiet and explosive eruptions occur in the same volcano? Then a <u>composite cone</u> is formed. During a quiet eruption, lava forms a wide base. An explosive eruption adds a layer of dust, ash, and rock particles. After many quiet and explosive eruptions, a very high cone is formed. The cone is wide with steep sides.

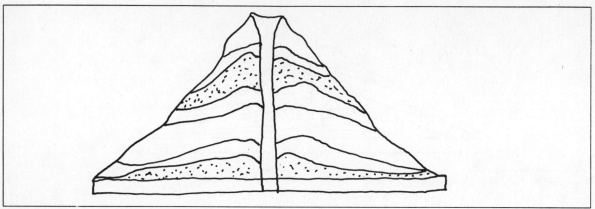

Figure C   *Composite cone*

MATCHING

Match each term in Column A with its description in Column B. Write the correct letter in the space provided.

	Column A		Column B
_____	1. crater	a)	gentle slopes
_____	2. composite cone	b)	steep sides with narrow bases
_____	3. cinder cone	c)	opening from which lava flows
_____	4. shield cone	d)	steep sides with wide bases
_____	5. vent	e)	funnel-shaped pit

In the space provided, classify each volcano as "quiet" or "explosive."

1. _____ **2.** _____

Figure D

Figure E

In the spaces provided, identify the kind of volcano shown in each drawing. Use the terms shield cone, cinder cone, and composite cone. Then answer the questions.

Figure F

Figure G

Figure H

1. _____ **2.** _____ **3.** _____

4. What material makes up a shield cone? _____

5. Does a shield cone form from a quiet eruption or an explosive eruption? _____

6. What kind of eruption forms a cinder cone? _____

7. What kind of eruptions form composite cones? _____

8. Which type of cone has the most narrow base? _____

WHAT DOES THE DIAGRAM SHOW?

The diagram below shows volcanoes, magma, and things that are part of volcanic action. Study the diagram. Then answer the questions below the diagram. Answer by writing the correct letters in the spaces provided.

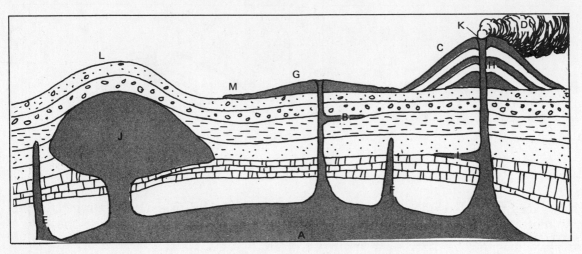

Figure I

1. explosive volcano _____

2. quiet volcano _____

3. lava flow _____

4. main magma supply _____

5. domed mountain _____

6. trapped magma that formed the domed mountain _____

7. poisonous gases, rocks, cinders, and ashes _____

8. crater _____

9. vent _____

You have not studied these parts. But see if you can find them from the descriptions.

10. Sometimes, trapped magma flows between rock layers. This flow is called a sill. The diagram shows two sills. What are their letters? _____

11. Trapped magma also flows upward between cracks in rocks. This flow is called a dike. Two dikes are labeled. What are their letters? _____

What are fossil fuels?

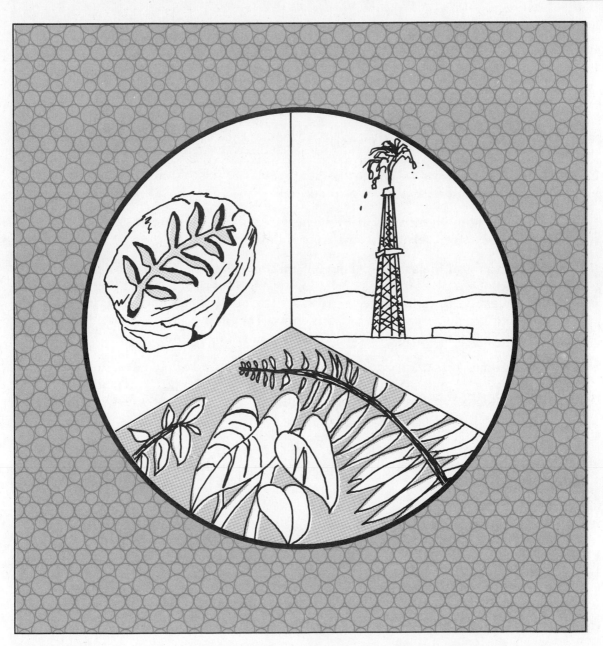

fossil fuels: natural fuels that come from the remains of living things

LESSON 28 | What are fossil fuels?

Most of the energy we use comes from **fossil fuels**. Coal, oil, and natural gas are fossil fuels. What is a fossil fuel?

A fuel is something we burn for energy. Not all fuels are fossil fuels. Fossil fuels are fuels that come from living things of the past.

How did fossil fuels form? About 325 million years ago, there were great swamps. Swamps are areas of shallow water with a lot of plant life.The land was warm. Thick forests grew. As the plants aged and died, they fell into the swamps. Other forests grew. They too grew old and died. Still other forests grew and fell. This happened over and over.

The fallen plants decayed. They formed a thick, muddy bog. After many, many years the decaying plant materials changed to <u>peat</u>. The peat became covered with sediment. After millions of years, the pressure of the sediment slowly changed the peat into coal.

Oil and natural gas also formed from once living things. Scientists believe that they were formed from decaying sea plants and animals.

Figure A

Plants that lived 325 million years ago became the coal that we use today.

1. What kind of energy do plants capture? _____

2. Where did the energy in coal come from originally?_____

Figure B

Scientists believe that 8 to 24 meters (20 to 80 feet) of plant material is needed to form a layer of coal just one-third of a meter (one foot) thick.

3. Why is coal found in layers?

_____

_____

_____

_____

Figure C

When sea plants and animals died, they were covered with sediments. The sediments changed into sedimentary rock. The decaying sea plants and animals changed to oil, or petroleum and natural gas. The oil moved with water through the cracks and holes in the rock. When it reached a layer it could not pass through, the oil began to collect. Oil is found mostly in anticlines.

Usually where there is oil, there is also natural gas.

MORE ABOUT COAL

There are four main kinds of coal. The most common are bituminous [bi-TEW-muh-nus] and anthracite [AN-thruh-syt]

• Bituminous coal is called "soft" coal.

• Anthracite coal is called "hard" coal.

• Bituminous coal is not really soft. It just is not as hard as anthracite coal.

• Anthracite coal gives more heat and burns with less smoke than bituminous coal.

The diagrams below show coal burning. One is bituminous. The other is anthracite.

Study the diagrams. Then answer the questions below.

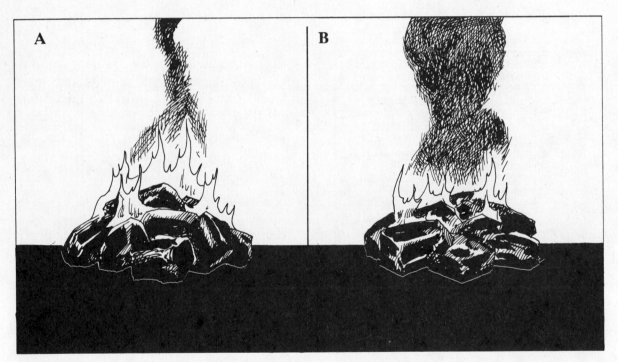

Figure D

1. Which fuel is anthracite coal? _____

2. Which fuel is bituminous coal? _____

3. Which one do you think releases more pollution? _____

4. Which one do you think releases less pollution? _____

5. Which coal is harder? _____

MULTIPLE CHOICE

In the space provided, write the letter of the word that best completes each statement.

_____ 1. We get energy by burning
   a) swamps.   b) fuel.
   c) sediment   d) electricity.

_____ 2. The energy in fuel came from
   a) gas.   b) electricity.
   c) the sun.   d) coal.

_____ 3. Coal comes from
   a) fuel.   b) sediment.
   c) molds.   d) plants.

_____ 4. Coal is a fossil fuel because
   a) it was formed a long time ago. b) it is found in layers.
   c) it comes from prehistoric plants and gives energy.
   d) it started as a bog.

_____ 5. Which of the following is not a fossil fuel?
   a) coal.   b) oil.
   c) uranium.   d) natural gas.

MATCHING

Match each term in Column A with its description in Column B. Write the correct letter in the space provided.

	Column A	Column B	
_____ 1.	bituminous	a)	coal, oil, natural gas
_____ 2.	anthracite	b)	start of coal
_____ 3.	fossil fuels	c)	soft coal
_____ 4.	peat	d)	where coal is found
_____ 5.	sedimentary rock layers	e)	hard coal

TRUE OR FALSE

In the space provided, write "true" if the sentence is true. Write "false" if the sentence is false.

_____ 1. All fuels supply energy.

_____ 2. All fuels are fossil fuels.

_____ 3. Coal is a fossil fuel.

_____ 4. Coal is the only fossil fuel.

_____ 5. All fuels give the same amount of energy.

_____ 6. Anthracite coal gives more energy than bituminous coal.

_____ 7. Natural gas is a fossil fuel.

_____ 8. Oil is made from decaying sea plants and animals.

_____ 9. It takes only a short time to form fossil fuels.

_____ 10. Wood is a fuel.

REACHING OUT

Look back at Figure C on Page 176. Why do you think the water, oil, and gas are found in layers?

_____

_____

_____

_____

How do toxic wastes affect the environment?

29

pollutants [puh-LOOT-ents]:   harmful substances
pollution [puh-LOO-shun]:   anything that harms the environment

LESSON 29 | How do toxic wastes affect the environment?

Since the beginning of human history, people have been changing their environment. Some changes have been helpful. Others have been harmful. Floods, for example may cause a great deal of hardships, and even death. Dams have been built to control floods. This, of course, is a good change. However, dams also change the local environment in bad ways. Farmlands are left infertile. Plant and fish life in streams may be destroyed.

Pollution [puh-LOO-shun] is a harmful result of human activity. Pollution is anything that harms the environment. Pollution occurs when harmful substances called **pollutants** [puh-LOOT-ents] are released into the environment.

You probably know that pollution is a major problem. It harms every part of the environment, the air, the water, and the land.

Pollution is a <u>worldwide</u> problem. Cooperation among all nations is needed to help stop pollution.

Toxic wastes are one group of pollutants. Toxic wastes are poisonous chemicals and chemical by-products. Some are radioactive too. Radioactive substances are known to cause cancer and birth defects.

Factories, and especially chemical plants, produce most toxic wastes. What happens to the toxic wastes? Some are dumped into lakes, rivers and oceans. Others are buried in drums in the ground. In many places, the drums have rusted and broken apart. The toxic wastes are leaking from the drums into the ground. The wastes pollute the soil. They also seep into our water supply. Certain wastes have contaminated food, and water supplies. This has killed living things.

In 1980, a law was passed to clean up toxic waste sites in the United States. However, the clean-up of toxic wastes is a difficult problem. Cleaning up toxic wastes is expensive and takes a lot of time.

WHAT DO THE PICTURES SHOW?

Study Figures A, B, and C. Then answer the questions on the lines provided.

Figure A

Figure B

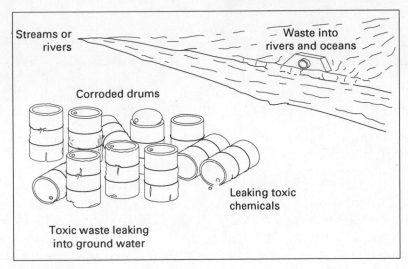

Figure C

1. Which figure shows toxic wastes being dumped directly into a lake?_____

2. **a)** What has happened to the drums in Figure C? _____

   _____

   b) What is happening to the toxic wastes in the drums? _____

   _____

3. Why is the person in Figure B Wearing a protective suit? _____

   _____

TOXIC WASTES

Trace the path toxic wastes may take in Figure A. Notice how they spread out in a web of damage and destruction. There are many possibilities.

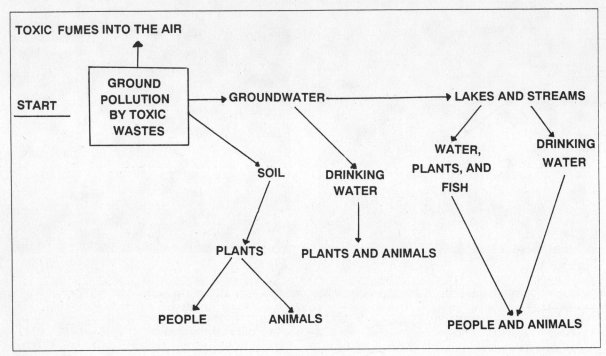

Figure D

Answer the questions about Figure D on the lines provided.

1. Toxic wastes can produce toxic _____ that escape into the air.

   fumes, water

2. Into what two things can toxic wastes leak?_____ and

   _____

3. Polluted ground water may be carried to _____ and _____ .

4. What living things are <u>directly</u> affected by the pollution of lakes and streams?

   _____

5. What living things are <u>directly</u> affected by soil pollution? _____

6. Where does our drinking water come from?_____

7. What living things eat plants and fish that are affected by toxic chemicals?

   _____

8. How do toxic wastes spread throughout the environment?_____

   _____

   _____

TRUE OR FALSE

In the space provided, write "true" if the sentence is true. Write "false" if the sentence is false.

_____ 1. Pollution is a worldwide problem.

_____ 2. The clean-up of toxic wastes is easy.

_____ 3. All toxic wastes are buried in the ground.

_____ 4. Toxic wastes only harm fish and water plants.

_____ 5. Pollution is anything that harms the environment.

_____ 6. Radioactive substances cause cancer and birth defects.

_____ 7. Toxic wastes do not produce fumes.

_____ 8. Toxic wastes pollute water and food supplies.

_____ 9. All human changes are bad.

_____ 10. Chemical plants produce most toxic wastes.

NUCLEAR ENERGY

Figure E

Today people are using up oil, coal, and natural gas at a very rapid rate. These are our main energy resources. Therefore, people are looking for other energy sources.

Nuclear energy is another source of energy. Today, nuclear power plants have been built in many places. However, there are drawbacks to using nuclear energy. Dangerous radioactive wastes are produced. Storing and getting rid of these wastes is a major problem.

How can radioactive wastes harm people? _____

_____

_____

CROSSWORD PUZZLE

Use the clues to complete the crossword puzzle.

Clues

Across

1. produce toxic chemicals

6. where toxic chemicals are buried

8. birth _____

9. to fix

11. an energy resource

12. gases

14. poisonous chemicals

Down

2. chemically weathered

3. place

4. change

5. harmful substances

7. control floods

10. store toxic wastes

11. can be caused by radioactive substances

13. to leak

What is relative age?
What is absolute age?

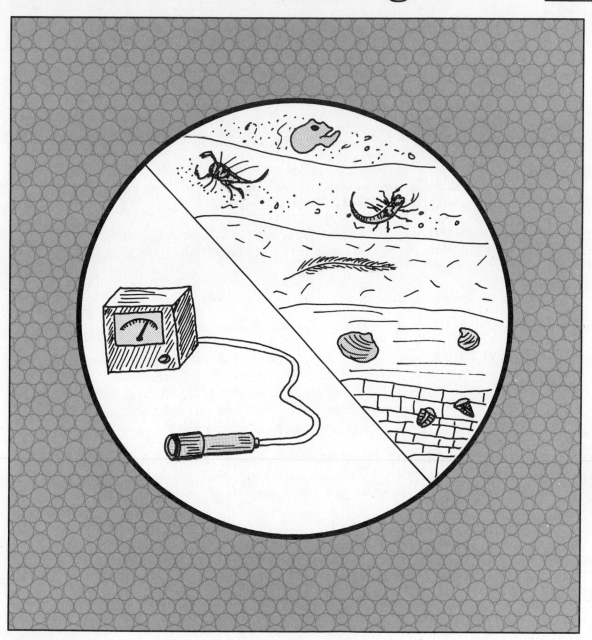

absolute age: specific age of a rock or fossil
fossil: remain, or trace, of a living thing that lived long ago
relative age: age of an object compared to the age of another object

LESSON 30

What is relative age?
What is absolute age?

How old is the earth? Scientists believe it is about 4 1/2 billion years old. However, they do not know that for sure. It is just an estimate, an educated guess, but probably a pretty good one.

How do we arrive at this number? The earth's age is estimated by dating its rocks. So far, the oldest rocks that have been found are about 4 1/2 billion years old.

How do we know the age of rocks?

Two kinds of dating are used—**relative dating** and **absolute dating.**

<u>Relative dating</u> does not give us an exact age. Relative age is the age of an object compared to the age of another object. It just compares the ages of different things. For example, you are older than a first-grader, but younger than your parents. The relative age of a rock tells scientists that one rock layer is older or younger than another rock layer.

<u>Absolute dating</u> gives an age in actual number of years. For example: 3 years old, 1000 years old, 2 million years old. Absolute age tells scientists the actual number of years ago a rock layer formed.

UNDERSTANDING RELATIVE AGE

To determine the relative age of rocks, scientists use a simple law of science. It says that younger rocks are found on top of older rocks.

The diagram below shows six rock layers. Study the layers. Then answer the questions below the diagram.

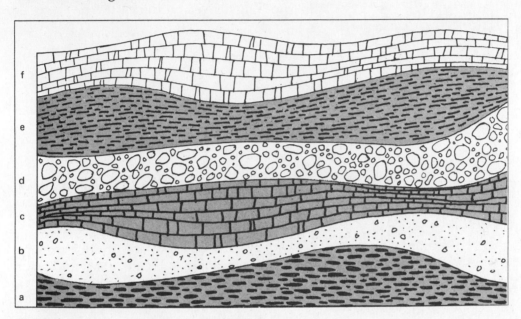

Figure A

1. Which is the oldest rock layer? _____

2. Which is the youngest rock layer? _____

3. Which layer was laid down last? _____

4. Which layer was laid down first? _____

5. Name the layers in order in which they were laid down. _____

6. Name the layers that are younger than layer d. _____

7. Name the layers that are older than layer d. _____

8. This method of dating rocks and fossils is _____
   absolute dating, relative dating

9. Relative age _____ tell age in "number of years."
   does, does not

10. What kind of rock is shown in the diagram? _____

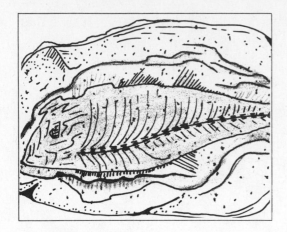

Figure B *Fossils*

Scientists also use **fossils** to help find the relative age of rock layers. Fossils are the remains, or traces, of living things that lived long ago. A fossil can be a bone, a footprint, a shell, or even the whole body of an organism that no longer lives on the earth.

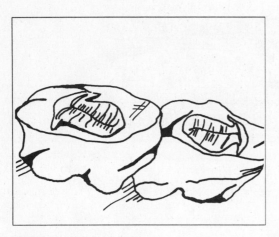

Figure C

Most fossils are found in sedimentary rock layers. Certain fossils can be used to help find the relative age of rock layers. These fossils are called index fossils. To be an index fossil, an organism must have lived only during a short part of the earth's history. Many fossils of the organisms have to be found in rock layers. The fossils must be found over a wide area of the earth.

Figure D *Graptolite*

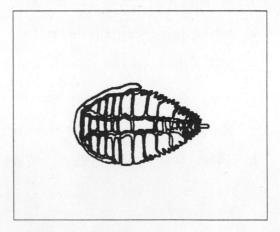

Figure E *Trilobite*

Graptolites [GRAP-tuh-lites] and trilobites [TRY-luh-bites] are two index fossils. These two organisms lived in the oceans. Graptolites lived 350–450 million years ago. Trilobites lived 500–600 million years ago. If scientists find a rock layer with trilobite fossils in it, they know that the rock layer is older than any layer with graptolite fossils.

Study the rock layers and fossils in Figure F. Then answer the questions below the diagram.

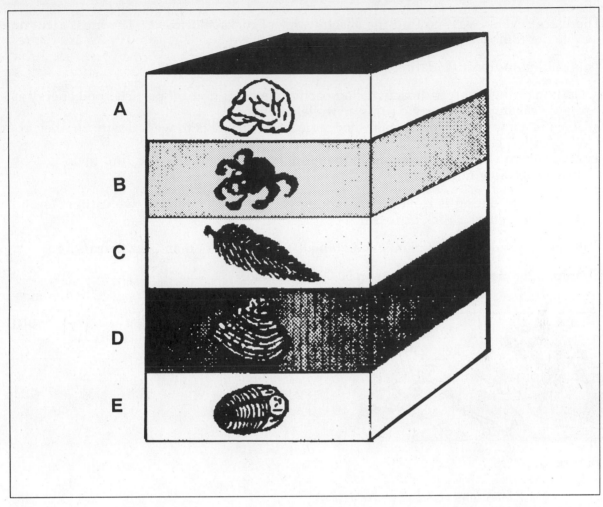

Figure F

1. Which rock layer is about 500–600 million years old? _____

2. How do you know? _____

_____

_____

3. Which rock layer is about 350–450 million years old? _____

4. How do you know? _____

_____

_____

5. What is an index fossil? _____

_____

_____

There are several ways to find the absolute age of rocks and fossils. The most accurate way is the radioactive method.

This is how radioactive dating works:

- Certain elements are radioactive. Radioactive elements give off particles and energy as they wear down. As they do this, new elements form.
- Scientists know how long it takes for radioactive elements to wear down. So, they are like natural clocks.
- Radioactive elements are found in many rocks and fossils. We can find their ages by measuring how much these elements have worn down.

Most absolute dating is done by measuring the amount of radioactive carbon 14 and uranium 238 left in a rock or fossil.

Carbon 14 dates fossils *of* plants and animals that lived less than 50,000 years ago.

Uranium 238 dates rocks older than 50,000 years old.

This instrument is called a *Geiger* [GY-gur] *counter*. It measures radioactivity.

Figure G

Answer these questions about absolute dating.

1. Radioactive dating give the _____ of a rock.
   relative age, absolute age

2. Radioactive dating _____ tell age in number of years.
   does, does not

3. Name two radioactive elements. _____ _____

4. Which radioactive element is used to date rocks? _____

5. Which radioactive element is used to date fossils? _____

6. Which radioactive element would you use to date the bones of an animal that lived

   less than 50,000 years ago? _____

7. Which radioactive element would you use to date a rock millions of years old?

   _____

8. Name an instrument that measures radioactivity. _____

FILL IN THE BLANK

Complete each statement using a term or terms from the list below. Write your answers in the spaces provided. Some words may be used more than once.

older   trilobites   compares
radioactive   relative   graptolites
does not   younger   absolute
index

1. The two methods of dating rocks and fossils are called _____ dating

   and _____ dating.

2. Relative dating _____ tell actual age.

3. Relative dating _____ the ages of different rocks.

4. Two words used in relative dating are _____ and _____ .

5. Absolute dating gives _____ age.

6. Fossils used to help date rocks are called _____ fossils.

7. Absolute dating uses _____ elements.

8. Two index fossils are _____ and _____ .

9. Top rock layers are _____ than layers below them.

10. Bottom rock layers are _____ than layers above them.

MATCHING

Match each term in Column A with its description in Column B. Write the correct letter in the space provided.

Column A

_____ 1. relative dating

_____ 2. absolute dating

_____ 3. uranium 238

_____ 4. carbon 14

_____ 5. Geiger counter

Column B

a) gives age in "number of years"

b) dates dead plants and animals less than 50,000 years old

c) measures radioactivity

d) age is described as "younger or older than"

e) dates rocks older than 50,000 years old

SCIENCE *EXTRA*

Geologist

Do you like the outdoors? Do you like to travel? If you do, you may want to consider a career in geology.

We rely upon geologists and their assistants, geological technicians, a great deal. Geologists spend much of their time searching for the natural resources society needs to function. Metal is used to make cars, planes, buildings, refrigerators, radios, jewelry and many of the things we use every day. All of these metals had to be mined from the earth. The oil, coal, and natural gas we use to generate electricity and produce gasoline also is obtained from the earth. Geologists often can locate these natural resources.

In their search for natural resources, geologists travel all over the world collecting rocks and fossil samples on the ground, under the ground, and at the bottom of the oceans. Geologists and geological technicians then analyze their samples to determine what elements and compounds are located where the sample is taken.

Most geologists are involved in a search for natural resources. However, there are many other types of research that geologists do. Many geologists study the earth today to try to figure out what the earth was like millions and even billions of years ago. Since most rocks change very slowly, the rocks that geologists study often are millions of years old. By studying fossils, geologists can even learn things about what life was like on earth a long time ago.

You need a bachelor's degree in science to become a geologist. Many geologists also have a master's degree or even a doctorate degree. The training to become a geological technician can be gained at a two year college or a technical school. In any case, you should have an active mind and body because geology is not just a job, it's an adventure.

What is the fossil record?

geologic [jee-uh-LAJ-ik] **time scale:** an outline of the major events in the earth's
history

LESSON 31 | What is the fossil record?

The "detectives" who have "read" fossil clues have put together the story of life on earth.

Fossils tell us much about the earth's history. Fossils show that many kinds of organisms lived at different times in the earth's history. The fossil record shows that life probably began in the water. The earliest living things were simple living things that lived in the sea. As time passed, more complex forms of life appeared. Some plants and animals began to live on land.

The fossil record also shows that many kinds of living things died out completely. They became extinct. The wooly mammoth, the trilobite [TRY-luh-bite], and the dinosaur are three extinct animals. There are fossils of about 130 thousand extinct living things.

Other forms of life did not become extinct. However, the fossil record shows they changed over time. And still other things that are alive today have not changed much since early times. Animals like snails, snakes, and cockroaches can be traced from early times. They have hardly changed.

The fossil record also shows that the earth's climate and surfaces have changed. For example, fossils of alligator-like animals have been found in Canada. Today, alligators live in warm climates. The fossils in Canada indicate that at some time in the earth's history, Canada had a warmer climate than it does today.

The fossil record is not complete. There are many gaps, or empty spaces. However, we now have a pretty clear story. We have been able to trace the major events in the earth's history and the development of most living things. In addition, we have been able to trace the development of human beings.

HOW THE HORSE DEVELOPED

Everyone knows what a horse looks like, but the horse did not always look like it does today. The diagrams below show how the horse has changed. It took about 60,000,000 years for the horse to develop. Here's a surprise. The earliest horse was only about 61 centimeters (24 inches) tall.

early horse

modern horse

Figure A

Study the diagrams in Figure A. What changes do you see? Fill in the correct answers on the lines provided.

1. The horse _____ grown in size.

has, has not

2. The legs have become _____ .

shorter, longer

3. The early horse _____ toes.

had, did not have

4. The modern horse _____ toes.

has, does not have

A cow eats only plants. A cow's teeth are mostly flat. A tiger eats only meat. A tiger's teeth are mostly pointed. The teeth of a modern horse are mostly flat.

5. What do you think modern horses eat?_____

TIMETABLE OF LIFE ON EARTH

By studying rocks and fossils, scientists have developed a **geologic** [jee-uh-LAJ-ik] **time scale**. The scale is an outline of major events in the earth's history. The scale lists four eras of our planet. It tells about how long ago each one began and about how long it lasted.

Study the chart. Then answer the questions on the next page. (Hint: Read this chart from the bottom up.)

ERA	BEGAN ABOUT	LASTED ABOUT	IMPORTANT FORMS OF LIFE
Cenozoic recent life	65 million years ago	65 million years (to present)	Modern humans, cattle, modern horse, apes and monkeys. Flowering plants spread.
Mesozoic middle life	225 million years ago	160 million years	Huge dinosaurs rule the earth-then become extinct. First birds and mammals. First flowering plants.
Paleozoic ancient life	600 million years ago	375 million years	Fish. First land animals (amphibians), and then early reptiles. Insects. Trilobites and many other sea animals with shells. Coal-forming period. Early land seed plants, then thick swamp forests.
Precambrian early life	4.5 billion years ago	3.9 billion years	Only simple sealife. One-celled living things called bacteria.

Figure B

WHICH ERA?

Name the era...

1. that started 6.5 million years ago? _____

2. that started about 4.5 billion years ago? _____

3. that lasted the longest? _____

4. in which we live? _____

5. during which dinosaurs lived? _____

6. during which the simplest life forms developed? _____

7. during which flowering plants first grew? _____

8. during which the first land animals lived? _____

9. in which insects first appeared? _____

10. in which early reptiles developed? _____

11. in which there was only sea life? _____

12. in which the dinosaurs died out? _____

13. in which birds first developed? _____

14. in which apes first developed? _____

15. which lasted about 375 million years? _____

MATCHING

Match each term in Column A with its description in Column B. Write the correct letter in the space provided.

	Column A	Column B
_____	1. wooly mammoth	a) where life began
_____	2. sedimentary rocks	b) had four toes
_____	3. the sea	c) where most fossils are found
_____	4. early horse	d) earliest forms of life
_____	5. bacteria	e) extinct

TRUE OR FALSE

In the space provided, write "true" if the sentence is true. Write "false" if the sentence is false.

_____ **1.** Fossils are traces of past life.

_____ **2.** Animals are the only kind of life.

_____ **3.** There has been life on earth for billions of years.

_____ **4.** Life began on land.

_____ **5.** All organisms moved from the sea to land.

_____ **6.** The fossil record shows the earth's climate has changed.

_____ **7.** As time passed, more complicated life developed.

_____ **8.** Many kinds of plants and animals have changed a lot.

_____ **9.** Snails and snakes have changed a lot.

_____ **10.** Fossils help us understand how people developed.

WHICH CAME FIRST?

In each of the pairs below, one of the things came before the other. On the line next to each pair, write the name of the thing that came before the other. (To answer this, use the Geologic Time Scale on page 196.)

1. bacteria or trilobites? _____

2. fishes or birds? _____

3. frogs or birds? _____

4. flowering plants or seed plants? _____

5. people or dinosaurs? _____

6. land animals or sea animals? _____

7. cockroaches or birds? _____

8. birds or monkeys? _____

9. complicated life or sample life? _____

10. bacteria or fungi? _____

THE METRIC SYSTEM

METRIC-ENGLISH CONVERSIONS

	Metric to English	English to Metric
Length	1 kilometer = 0.621 mile (mi)	1 mi = 1.61 km
	1 meter = 3.28 feet (ft)	1 ft = 0.305 m
	1 centimeter = 0.394 inch (in)	1 in = 2.54 cm
Area	1 square meter = 10.763 square feet	1 ft^2 = 0.0929 m^2
	1 square centimeter = 0.155 square inch	1 in^2 = 6.452 cm^2
Volume	1 cubic meter = 35.315 cubic feet	1 ft^3 = 0.0283 m^3
	1 cubic centimeter = 0.0610 cubic inches	1 in^3 = 16.39 cm^3
	1 liter = .2642 gallon (gal)	1 gal = 3.79 L
	1 liter = 1.06 quart (qt)	1 qt = 0.94 L
Mass	1 kilogram = 2.205 pound (lb)	1 lb = 0.4536 kg
	1 gram = 0.0353 ounce (oz)	1 oz = 28.35 g
Temperature	Celsius = 5/9 (°F –32)	Fahrenheit = 9/5°C + 32
	0°C = 32°F (Freezing point of water)	72°F = 22°C (Room temperature)
	100°C = 212°F	98.6°F = 37°C
	(Boiling point of water)	(Human body temperature)

METRIC UNITS

The basic unit is printed in capital letters.

Length	Symbol
Kilometer	km
METER	m
centimeter	cm
millimeter	mm

Area	Symbol
square kilometer	km^2
SQUARE METER	m^2
square millimeter	mm^2

Volume	Symbol
CUBIC METER	m^3
cubic millimeter	mm^3
liter	L
milliliter	mL

Mass	Symbol
KILOGRAM	kg
gram	g

Temperature	Symbol
degree Celsius	°C

SOME COMMON METRIC PREFIXES

Prefix		Meaning
micro-	=	0.000001, or 1/1,000,000
milli-	=	0.001, or 1/1000
centi-	=	0.01, or 1/100
deci-	=	0.1, or 1/10
deka-	=	10
hecto-	=	100
kilo-	=	1000
mega-	=	1,000,000

SOME METRIC RELATIONSHIPS

Unit	Relationship
kilometer	1 km = 1000 m
meter	1 m = 100 cm
centimeter	1 cm = 10 mm
millimeter	1 mm = 0.1 cm
liter	1 L = 1000 mL
milliliter	1 mL = 0.001 L
tonne	1 t = 1000 kg
kilogram	1 kg = 1000 g
gram	1 g = 1000 mg
centigram	1 cg = 10 mg
milligram	1 mg = 0.001 g

GLOSSARY/INDEX

magma [MAG-muh]: molten rock inside the earth, 51

mantle: thick layer of rock below the crust and above the core, 25 •

mass: amount of matter in an object, 1

mechanical [muh-KAN-ih-kul] weathering: weathering in which the chemical make up of rocks does not change, 75

metamorphic [met-uh-MOWR-fik] rock: rock that forms from pieces of other rocks or the remains of once-living things, 63

mid-ocean ridge: underwater mountain chain, 129

minerals: natural solids formed from elements and compounds in the earth's crust, 31

moraine [moor-AYN]: ridge of till deposited by a retreating glacier, 101

ore: mineral that is mined because it contains useful metals or nonmetals, 37

plain: large flat area not much higher than sea level, 137

plateau [pla-TOH]: large flat region with higher elevation than a plain, 137

pollutants [puh-LOOT-ents]: harmful substances, 179

pollution [puh-LOO-shun]: anything that harms the environment, 179

relative age: age of an objet compared to the age of another object, 185

rock: natural solid that is made up of mineral grains stuck together, 31

rock cycle: series of natural processes by which rocks are slowly changed from one kind of rock to another, 69

runoff: rainwater that flows into streams and rivers, 87

safety alert symbols: signs that warn of hazards or dangers, 15

scientific method: problem solving guide, 9

sea arch: gap formed when waves cut completely through a section of rock, 113

sea cave: hollowed out part of a sea cliff, 113

sea cliff: steep rock face caused by wave erosion, 113

sea-floor spreading: process that froms new sea-floor, 129

sea level: average level of the water in the oceans, 155

sea stack: column of rock remaining after the collapse of a sea arch, 113

sedimentary [sed-uh-MEN-tuh-ree] rocks: rock that forms from pieces of other rocks or the remains of once-living things, 57

seismic [SYZ-mik] waves: earthquake waves, 161

streak: color of the powder left by a mineral, 43

syncline [SIN-klyn]: downward fold, 149

temperature: measure of how hot or cold something is, 1

theory of plate tectonics [tek-TAHN-iks]: theory that states the earth's crust is broken into pieces that float on the lower mantle, 129

till: rock material deposited by a glacier, 101

vent: opening from which lava flows, 167

volcano [vahl-KAY-noh]: vent and the pile of volcanic material around the vent, 167

volume: measure of the amount of space an object takes up, 1

weathering: breaking down of rocks and other materials on the earth's surface, 75

weight: measure of the pull of gravity on an object, 1